Essential Research Skills for Teens

Lucy Calkins, Series Editor

Mary Ehrenworth and Marc Todd

Photography by Peter Cunningham

Illustrations by Marjorie Martinelli

HEINEMANN ◆ PORTSMOUTH, NH

To our colleagues, past and present, at IS 289—the Hudson River Middle School, NYC

And to our partners, Rich Hallett, whose research in forest health and urban ecology has fueled our interest in the challenges of ethical research; and Cy Orfield, whose work in foster care for NYC's most vulnerable reminds us that equity and representation are critical lenses we must apply when looking at our students and the content we teach.

Heinemann
361 Hanover Street
Portsmouth, NH 03801–3912
www.heinemann.com

Offices and agents throughout the world

© 2019 by Lucy Calkins, Mary Ehrenworth, and Marc Todd

The authors and publisher wish to thank those who have generously given permission to reprint borrowed material:
"High School Tells Student to Remove Antiwar Shirt" from *The New York Times*. © 2003 The New York Times Company. All rights reserved. Used under license.

Cataloging-in-Publication data is on file with the Library of Congress.

ISBN-13: 978-0-325-11094-3

Editors: Anna Gratz Cockerille, Felicia O'Brien, and Kate Montgomery
Production: Elizabeth Valway
Cover and interior designs: Jenny Jensen Greenleaf
Photography: Peter Cunningham and André Martins
Illustrations: Marjorie Martinelli
Composition: Publishers' Design and Production Services, Inc.
Manufacturing: Steve Bernier

Printed in the United States of America on acid-free paper
23 22 21 20 19 VP 1 2 3 4 5

July 2019 printing

Contents

Registration instructions to access the digital resources that accompany this book may be found on p. xiv.

Acknowledgments

WE HAVE TO BEGIN by naming institutions that have shaped and contributed to this work from beginning to end. Those institutions include IS 289, the Hudson River School, which for many years was known as IS 89, until the vagaries of the New York City Department of Education gave this middle school another digit; Southridge High School, in Beaverton, Oregon; ASB, the American School of Barcelona; Avenues: the World School; Heinemann; and the Teachers College Reading and Writing Project.

Our work at IS 289 began about two decades ago, when the school first opened as a workshop school (in science, math, social studies, ELA, and the arts), and we thank founding principal Ellen Foote for how she questioned and probed every lesson we taught, every project we designed, and every text we put in front of kids. Ellen was that most formidable and fabulous of leaders, someone who made you want to be better, every day. One of Ellen's most insistent lenses was authenticity. When she looked down at some fake historical newspaper kids were happily creating in social studies, or she found kids dutifully filling in a worksheet in science, she would ask, "Is this what scientists or social scientists do?" We would cringe, and vow to do better. It's due to Ellen that we investigated how researchers and thinkers have used notebooks over the centuries, and we got rid of all things Xeroxed, and brought out the colored pencils, the notebooks, and mostly, the joy and beauty of reading and writing to think.

Ellen Foote's thought partner in the early days of IS 289 was Donna Santman, and her influence is felt here in the attention to critical literacies and to the ongoing work of helping adolescents work autonomously. Donna helped us to understand how the language and structure of instruction can affect the independence and clarity with which kids work.

Then there is the social studies and science team at IS 289. The work of our innovative colleagues, Julie Brown, Kara Buckley, Carol Shirai, and especially, Jaclyn Maricle, are poured into the nonfiction research skills and the notebook work you'll see in this unit. Kara and Jaclyn in particular helped develop the significance of synthesis pages in science. Carol Shirai and Patrick Hector's work helped students extend this work in social studies. Jaclyn is also extraordinarily gifted at creating tools and resources for students that help them work autonomously. We so admire how you lead in this work, Jaclyn. Keisha Adams, Jessica Collins, and Lori Coopersmith, your work with students with learning differences shows itself not only in the small-group work in this unit, but also in ways of thinking about multiple pathways for all kids.

Brian Gordon's work in sixth-grade science at 289 showed us how to help students begin this work, by getting kids to record data, keep track of information, and begin to write to interpret. Mari Mannino's work in seventh-grade science showed us that teachers can dive into this work immediately, if they trust students to learn from each other. Meanwhile the ELA team of Christina DiZebba, Heather Freyman, and Jennifer Brogan, especially their work with reading notebooks and teaching nonfiction reading skills, created opportunities for transfer for the kids, and for us. Chi-Man Ng and Yelena Berdichevsky showed us that high-level thinking skills can be fostered by workshop across the curriculum. We learn so much about instruction from your math classes. Gordon Ostrowski's work with the seventh-grade opera production has taught all of us at IS 289 about how hard kids will work when they are engaged in projects they care about deeply.

We love and admire the passion for content, for equity, and for learning that these teachers at IS 289 instill in their students, demonstrate in their own work, and share with colleagues. You'll see notebook work from all their students in the mentor text resources of this unit of study.

We have a special thank-you to some student leaders at IS 289, and that is the leaders of the GSA. These activists keep our minds turned toward issues of representation, of bias, and of microaggressions. They also help us see possibility, hope, and love. Thank you to Madeleine Ames, Olivia Baker, Tonya Jaffe, Mohamed Keussom, Sophia Lawsky, William Stein, and Jerson Yang.

Over the last few years, IS 289 has been gracefully led by Zeynep Ozkan and Andolyn Brown. These women have been dedicated to professional development and to increasing equity for students. Their zeal and also their practical, nose-to-the-schedule attention made all of this work possible. Zeynep, you supported our growth as educators, and were a leader we could turn to, as well as a thought partner and a collaborator. We love and admire you.

We are also grateful to Southridge High School, in Beaverton, Oregon, led by Principal David Lieslanik. David's leadership let us study the habits of teens who are highly successful academically. Visiting classrooms and talking to teens at Southridge and at Mountainside High School, both in Beaverton, Oregon, helped us clarify ways to help more teens with their studies. In this work, we have to do a shout-out to two extraordinary high school teachers at Southridge, English teacher Sharon Larpenteur and her teaching partner, history teacher Anne Karakas. Besides their avid love of dogs, which we share, these two women have honed workshop instruction in high school, giving us and our colleagues a vision of what IB and AP classes can look like when students have choice over what they read; when teachers model high-level thinking, reading, and writing work; and when student autonomy is prized.

To our friends at ASB, the American School at Barcelona, we say gracias, gràcies, y os saludamos! Thank you to Head of School, Mark Pingatore, for his intellectual leadership, and for inviting us to work alongside and inside this beautiful learning community. Thank you to Johanna Cena and Jenny Killion for the way they create an atmosphere where everyone wants to learn, and even more, for being such dear, dear friends. Thank you to Marta Lujan for showing us how workshop instruction thrives in multiple literacies. And for the work in this unit, we especially thank Jenny Killion, Lauren Freer, Lauren Gould, Dawn Austin, Tori Luthringer, and Kate Tighe for diving into notebook work with such passion and belief. Every time we get to work with you and your students, we come away changed. Thank you, as well, for hosting our secondary cohort, which brought us the wisdom of April Stout, coach extraordinaire at the American School of Madrid, and her team of teachers. We love working with you all.

We have learned an enormous amount from colleagues at Avenues: The World School, both through shared professional development and through vicarious learning through students and the work they've shared. Stephanie Shore's cutting-edge work with media literacies shows itself across the second bend of this unit, on ethical research and Internet literacy. Stephanie also showed us that students are deeply fascinated and troubled by issues in the world around them, and they will read and think deeply when given the opportunity. Ivan Cestero and Ron Widelac's work with teaching students to question historical perspectives helped us envision how students can disrupt dominant narratives in history. Michael Yarbrough showed us how avidly students will research when they care about their research topic. Mike Maccarone, Steven Carpenter, and Warren Tappe helped us build a vision of how kids will continue to read and research outside of school when their science teachers make science fascinating. And Todd Shy and Jordan Kravitz continue to help us see the contagious beauty of passion as a pedagogy.

To our colleagues at Heinemann, we thank you not only on our behalf, but on behalf of teachers everywhere, who may not know how many weekends, late nights, and extra effort go into these curricular tools. The work of Heinemann is more than publishing. It is intense care for kids, for equity, and for possibility. Thank you to Abby Heim, program director, for being a believer in and supporter of these units of study. Abby, you have been a pillar for us over these years and we are so grateful. Thank you to Anna Cockerille for editing and publishing, and being there for us every step of the way. We love your eager, quick intelligence, Anna. Thank you to Felicia O'Brien for reading so closely and solving so many tricky issues in the text—you made this unit so much clearer and more focused. Thank you to Elizabeth Valway, production editor extraordinaire, who shepherds the manuscript from where we compose in Google Docs to the version you now hold in your hands. Thank you to Shannon Thorner for taking such good care of the online resources, which are such an important part of this unit. Thank you to Peter Cunningham, for being a gorgeous, intimate, sensitive photographer, especially of teens. And a huge thank you to Lisa Bingen, who travels with us to conferences, shares our learning, helps in every possible way, and most importantly, believes in middle and high school units of study. Thank you as well to her team, especially Ashley Puffer.

Now we come to our colleagues at the Teachers College Reading and Writing Project. Over our many years of shared professional development, think tanks, and thinking-over-wine-or-in-airports, it has become impossible to separate where new ideas originate or whose brilliance infused a particular tool.

We know that the middle and secondary school team, led by our treasured friend Audra Robb, and including Cornelius Minor, Katy Wischow, Emily Strang-Campbell, Heather Burns, Pablo Wolfe, Laurie Burke, Kathleen Schechter, Dwight McCaulsky, Tim Steffen, Cheney Munson, Mandy Ehrlich, Janet Steinberg, David Keck, and Sonja Cherry-Paul, has tried these lessons, given us ideas for tools, questioned us, and laughed with us. This group's collective interest in and belief in adolescents fuels all our work. We still miss our middle school colleagues Chris Lehman, Kate Roberts, and Maggie Beattie Roberts, and their innovative thinking continues to push our work, especially their work on increasing student engagement. The same is true for Stacey Fell. Stacey's inspiring notebook work shows itself in these pages. We miss you at TCRWP but love having access to your classroom at Thompkins Square, Stacey, and we feel like you and Carole Mashameshesh are part of our intellectual and friendship team—thank you to both of you! Audra's leadership and friendship has been a mainstay for our work in schools and in our writing. Audra reads and thinks and questions and supports. We couldn't do any of this work without her. We love you, Audra.

The truth is that everyone at TCRWP informs this work and all our work, because the institution is a think tank. The work that Katie Clements and Kelly Boland Hohne have done in nonfiction reading lives in this unit of study. Sonja Cherry Paul's incisive, on-point analysis of pedagogy, teaching resources, and literature continually helps us in our mission to teach, understand, and support *all* students, and you will feel it in this unit as well. Every staff developer has intersected with our work at some point. As have our fabulous office staff, led by Lisa Cazzola and Rebecca Godlewicz, who make our institutes possible, and that's where we learn with teachers. Mary Ann Mustac researches and brings in outside speakers, who give us new knowledge. Suzanne Korn turns tools and documents into works of art. Amanda Hartman visits schools and regularly gives us her perspective of middle school

classrooms. Laurie Pessah not only leads the organization, she works with principals in ways that help us understand the challenges of provisioning classrooms and leading the work. Marjorie Martinelli needs special mention, as she designs the charts, leads the art department, and graces us with her competence, her care, and her insight. Colleen Cruz's work with both nonfiction reading and digital reading skills continues to alert us to how much work there is to do in this field—how many legitimate challenges kids face as they read digitally. We love her new book, *Writers Read Better: Nonfiction*, which has some brilliant lessons on reading digital nonfiction.

And then there is Lucy Calkins, founder and director of TCRWP. Lucy has been a series editor on these units of study, which means countless conversations, reading of manuscripts, and collaborative writing. Lucy has lived her professional life in the belief that helping kids become powerful readers and writers is an act of social justice. We salute that belief and hope that we live up to it.

For this book, we have a particular thank-you to Kate Montgomery, our editor. Kate acted as a thought partner from beginning to end. So much of what is new in this unit, in terms of what we want to teach kids about ethical research, comes from Kate, from her ideas, her responsiveness, her thoughtfulness. Kate has lived and taught and researched all over the world. Her concern for curriculum that forwards social justice, and her belief that pedagogy can affect kids' ethics, grounds this work.

We want to finish with love and gratitude to our partners. Rich Hallett talks to us about the challenges in science right now, shares his research, listens to our ideas, and most importantly, lets us live the kinds of lives where we can write. Cy Orfield provides a space for us to explore, plan, create, and reflect. All of this is essential to develop in our schools the kind of classrooms our students deserve. We adore you both.

An Orientation to the Unit

"Google" is not a synonym for "research."
—Dan Brown

 Research is formalized curiosity. It is poking and prying with a purpose.
—Zora Neale Hurston

WELCOME! THIS UNIT OF STUDY for social studies, science, and English language arts (ELA) teachers is exciting—and challenging too, in the best of ways. We have never seen students rise to the work with such enthusiasm as they did in the pilots of this unit, often surprising their teachers by bringing to light brilliant new ways of being media savvy and by being thrilled to get even savvier. (After all, which teens aren't happy to become more expert than their elders?) This unit is all about learning well in today's world and then sharing that knowledge with others—the most fundamental and joyous of human intellectual experiences. We hope you enjoy it as much as we have.

In this unit of study, you'll engage students in forming study groups to research a topic of contemporary and/or scientific or historical significance. The first bend is an immersion in essential study habits. In this bend your students will learn to build background knowledge independently, to function as effective study partners, and to keep powerful research notes. In the next two bends of the unit, your students will move into critical literacy skills: learning to research authors and groups as well as content; studying how search engines and the Internet respond to research; and becoming more alert to connotative language, confirmation bias, and fake news. As they gain expertise in their topics, students will also begin to study the disputes and arguments inside their topics, coming eventually to informed positions, which they will present in flash-debates and then in TED-style talks.

A Summary of Teaching inside *Essential Research Skills for Teens*			
		What will students learn to do?	**What will students make or do?**
BEND I	**Essential Study Habits**	Build background knowledge independently Be an effective study partner Take lean and effective research notes	**Infographic** explaining the context of an issue or topic
BEND II	**Critical Literacy Skills**	Research authors, sources, and content Take deeper, more comprehensive notes Work with search engines' non-neutrality Note, and compensate for confirmation bias Research sources and discern "fake news"	**Flash-debate** both sides of an argument
BEND III	**Turning Research into Activism**	Analyze a mentor text for purpose, structure, and craft Structure and craft their research and points Practice public-speaking skills	**Teen "TED talk"** to present a position, to bring others to a shared stance on an argument

We've chosen to focus on the skills in this unit because we believe they are the most essential study skills you can instill in your students. In high schools in which the Reading and Writing Project consults, we've done informal studies of students' work processes. These studies included analysis of the students' work and interviews with the students themselves. Many of the students were engaged in challenging academic classes, such as Advanced Placement and International Baccalaureate classes. We found that students who do very well academically share similar study habits. One is that these students do more outside of school—they read up on topics, they watch content videos, they talk to people about what they're studying. All of that interest and agency leads to increased background knowledge. We want to make sure that access to background knowledge is something *all* students know how to build, independently.

These successful students have another important study habit: they know how to get and be a study partner. That is, they have—and have built up—a combination of social intelligence and academic intelligence that Malcolm Gladwell describes in *Outliers*. Think back to when you took hard classes in high school or college or university. Chances are, you formed study groups. It's why Harvard Business School's curriculum is built around collaborative study groups—combining people's skill sets makes people stronger. Again, we want to help all students learn how to become a study partner, so they can contribute their strengths to others, and learn alongside them.

It's probably no surprise that a third crucial study habit is note-taking. Almost all the kids we interviewed had fabulous notebooks. We use the word *notebook* as a metaphor for wherever one takes notes—it might be an iPad, and for some kids it was a binder. Students or teachers can decide to go digital, though we use paper notebooks in this unit. It turns out that the neurons for innovation and creativity are activated when we work by hand. "When we write, a unique neural circuit is automatically activated," said Stanislas Dehaene, a psychologist at the Collège de France in Paris (*New York Times*, "What's Lost as Handwriting Fades" June 2, 2014). The mode of note-taking doesn't matter much (paper or on a screen), as long as it allows sketching and diagramming, rather than only typing. Though most of all, what we found matters is that kids go back into their notes. That kind of recursive quality to note-taking turns out to be a game changer.

We are really excited to instill these study habits in kids, so that more kids have access to the hardest academic classes, and more kids understand and develop the skill sets that will let them be successful in high school

and college. We're also excited to tackle critical Internet literacies. We were deeply embarrassed when piloting this unit to discover that one of the texts we included in the unit was a highly biased text—it's been moved out of Session 1 now! It was a high school student who suggested that this text might be fake news, and he gave us a protocol from a senior-level media literacy class taught by Stephanie Shore to assess the reliability of news items. That experience motivated us to tackle teaching kids the challenges of Internet research, especially how the Internet researches us, so that we end up only being exposed to sources that confirm our beliefs and biases.

It's a fraught experience to truly grapple with the perils of digital media access—and it's really important. Our kids, future voters all, are exposed to huge amounts of media. Your students will emerge from this unit better prepared to filter that media.

In terms of a final project, you have various choices. If you are pairing this unit of study with a writing unit, such as our unit of study on argument essays or position papers, then your final project will probably be an argument essay of some kind. The second bend of this unit leads students into ethical research, so that students research all sides of an argument, before coming to an informed position that acknowledges complexity and counterclaims.

You don't always need to turn a reading unit into a writing unit, however. Here, we suggest that students shift from background research to researching an argument related to their topic. Their research, which becomes more focused, leads students to an informed position, which they'll share in a collaborative TED-style talk. TED talks are engaging, quick to produce, and significant in current media. They'll give your students a chance to take up activists' positions, raising their voices about issues important to them.

OVERVIEW

Bend I: Essential Study Habits—Building Background Knowledge, Taking Lean Notes, and Becoming an Effective Study Partner

In Bend I of the unit, you'll instill the deep study habits that will help your students be successful in high school and college. You'll begin with a read-aloud that leads students to consider how more complex nonfiction teaches implicit as well as explicit ideas. Students will begin their research in study groups, which they'll maintain across the unit of study. Each study group will study a topic together, and in this bend, the group will work collaboratively to build background knowledge. That means that readers need to immerse themselves in their topic, reading fast and furious. You'll teach students, then, to take lean notes to read more, and to process much of what they learn through talk with a partner (a partner from inside their study group).

Along the way, besides teaching students to build background knowledge rapidly, you'll also be engaging students in an inquiry of how to be an effective study partner. You'll consider the role of introverts and extroverts, and you'll build a repertoire of ways that students can contribute to a study group.

Two important skills that you'll teach in this bend, along with lean note-taking, are vocabulary collection and synthesis notes. You'll see that we rely on Elfrieda Hiebert's research on vocabulary acquisition, which suggests that rather than frontloading vocabulary (which privileges memorization), instead, students should acquire vocabulary terms from their reading, and they work with these terms through a variety of conceptual sorts (which privileges conceptual understanding). Then, building on our research on successful high school students, which shows that students who go back into their notes learn more as well as do more thinking about what they've learned, you'll teach students to create synthesis pages and then infographics to consolidate their knowledge. We suggest some software tools for infographics—though of course students can work by hand if it's faster and easier. The goal is for students to pull together what they've learned so far, and teach others, using their consolidated notes.

Bend II: Ethical Research Practices and Internet Literacy

In Bend II of the unit, you'll launch with another read-aloud that leads students to consider the internal disputes and arguments inside of topics. Study groups, then, will consider the arguments inside of their topics that they find relevant and fascinating—and researchable. As they go off to research with this narrower focus, you'll teach students that ethical research doesn't involve researching only one side of an argument. Instead, ethical researchers find out more about multiple sides and perspectives. You'll teach students to keep a continuum of their sources, so they can assess the fairness of their research.

Students' note-taking practices need to deepen as they do more focused research. We've provided a set of mentor notebooks, from science and social studies and ELA research classes in middle and high school, for students to study. Usually this kind of inquiry inspires students to take their own

note-taking more seriously, as they see how other students diagram, annotate, sketch, and write to hold onto information and develop new thinking.

Once students are researching and note-taking with zeal and focus, you'll lead them into a deep study of bias—bias inside of texts, bias in search engines, and bias in the researcher. You'll teach students to study connotative language, to research authors and groups and their agendas, and to be alert to the non-neutrality of search engines. Finally, you'll coach students to be alert to the possibility of fake news, so they are more alert to distortion in the media they consume.

You'll finish the bend with flash-debates, in which students test out the positions they've come to through their research. Think ahead to which students are good at arguing, because you'll need students who can argue both sides for these debates, even if they are going to ultimately support one side. Arguing the opposite side helps researchers consider counterclaims and alternate perspectives. The goal of these debates is not only to help students strengthen their evidence-based argument skills. It's to move them from arguing to win to arguing to learn.

Bend III: From Research to Activism

Bend III is a short bend, and its goal is to give students an opportunity to turn their research into activism. The bend begins with a read-aloud, which is an inquiry into teen TED talks. Students will watch some TED talks given by teens to think about how TED talks go—their purpose and structure and craft. Then they'll work with their study group to think through how their own talk might go. We suggest that your students' TED talks will be three minutes in length—long enough to say something significant, and short enough that they need to sort through their research and make choices about what to include.

The structure of TED talks is less formal than many of the argument essays that are written for school, and you'll help students grapple with structure, so that study groups can work on developing an underlying structure for their talks. Then you'll have a day of centers, in which students can choose to study the parts of successful TED talks (a return to structure), public-speaking skills, and/or craft techniques of this genre.

You'll wrap up the unit with your students delivering their TED talks. We've taught these kinds of quick TED talks a lot, and so we give some pointed advice in the letter for this session on ways to structure the filming, the audience role, and so on. We also provide some assessment tools for the

TED talks and for student notebooks, for the end of the unit. The TED talk celebration will be somewhat messy and also inspiring, as you see your students speak up about issues they know a lot about and care a lot about. Think ahead about whether you want to invite others to these talks.

ASSESSMENT

We've provided two assessment tools for this unit, both to support analysis of the research notebook work: a student-facing checklist and a more detailed, teacher-facing rubric. You can find both on the online resources.

We suggest that at the end of Bend I, students self-assess their research notebooks for the first three items on the checklist. You might also collect your students' research notebooks around this time and also assess for these three qualities. Near or at the end of Bend II, you can follow the same protocol for items 4, 5, and 6. Near or at the end of Bend III, you can assess item 7. This way, you won't have to assess all of your students' notebook work at one time, and students will also get feedback along the way.

It can be challenging to assess kids' nonfiction reading skills, particularly at the higher levels. The work they do is so complex and invisible. You'll see that the rubric we've provided to assess kids' notebook work is also meant to help you assess critical thinking and reading research skills. Here, we think that a legitimate way to assess kids' reading skills is to study what they've included in their research notes.

There are of course, alternate ways kids could show their learning. It may be that some kids can film themselves talking about their topic. Some of our science teacher colleagues have made videotaping an option, and kids who do not produce much writing now have a way to demonstrate that they've learned a lot. Consider asking your kids how they might best show the thinking they've done.

GETTING READY

There are essential parts of getting ready for this unit that will be particularly helpful for you and your students. We suggest that you think about: preparing text sets, creating partnerships, organizing your space to support your students as they research, marking up and rehearsing the read-aloud, and preparing your research notebook.

Preparing What Kids Will Read—Research Text Sets

As you look ahead to this unit, we suggest you familiarize yourself with the topics and issues that we provided for you in our online resources. Our online resources have been strategically curated to include a combination of both video and shorter articles. In addition, we suggest that you supplement our online resources with copies of trade books for each topic and issue by talking with your school librarian and reaching out to content area teachers. Keep in mind it is well worth seeking out a few easier texts for your students, so they can build on the knowledge from those to access increasingly harder texts.

We've prepared digital text sets on eighteen topics, six each inside the categories of historical topics, civics issues, and science topics. We suggest that you use these text sets as starter sets, knowing that the goal is for kids to spend lots of time reading, not lots of time surfing the Internet. Of course, you can create your own text sets on other topics, especially local ones. Our colleagues in Seattle, for instance, have created text sets on salmon fishing, our colleagues in Japan have looked at whaling, and so on. If you want to share your text sets, or ask about others, the Units of Study Facebook page is a great resource.

Historical Topics	Contemporary Civics Issues	Science Studies
• Immigration	• Immigration bias	• Plastics pollution
• Free speech	• Racial bias	• Ecosystem preservation
• Voting rights	• Gun violence	• Fishing rights
• Segregation	• War on drugs	• Green energy choices
• Gun control	• Gender and sexual identity equity	• Water rights
• Rights of indigenous peoples	• Climate change	• Climate change

We've organized these text sets as padlets—visually compelling digital archives. They're easy to create, and if your school pays for an account, you can make unlimited numbers of them. You can start them, and kids can add to them. Students can access padlets on any digital device, from a phone to a laptop. Padlets also let you annotate resources, in a digital annotated bibliography. They're quite flexible.

We focused on including texts that would be interesting and accessible for teens. All texts are downloadable. You may want to print some of the texts as well, so that if online access is problematic, there are always texts for kids to read. It's up to you whether you want to dive deeply into civics, history, or science, or if you want to offer a range of these topics for students.

For Day Zero—"Forming Research Clubs and Choosing Research Topics," it may work best to have only two or three texts available on each topic. We recommend printing one or two of the articles from the online resources and paring with a single trade book. If digital access is very easy in your classroom, then include a video as well, otherwise, you might stick to print just for this day. Limiting the texts on Day Zero allows students to preview the variety of topics to determine what seems significant, important, and meaningful to them, without getting into the vaster array of texts that will be available across the unit.

If you are giving students access to the entire text set for each topic, you might also have a card made, with a couple of shorter or more accessible texts suggested for previewing.

Creating Partnerships and Then Study Groups

Across the unit, your students will benefit from being in effective partnerships. You can think about these partnerships in two ways. First, you can pair students in same-level partnerships. Partners reading at similar levels encounter shared complexities in the texts they read. You can increase your reach by conferring with both partners together about strategies that fit with those text complexities.

Another way to orchestrate partnerships is to let students pick their own partners. Students will often choose a partner with shared interests and passion for research. You can confer with these about high-leverage research habits. Both types of partnerships have value. You have to decide what leverage you want from the partnerships for this unit.

Keep in mind that you may have one or two students who could benefit from extra support—or your class may have an odd number of students. In that case, you might consider creating one or two groups of three students. We find that a deliberate group of three students can be just as effective as a partnership. We sometimes suggest pairing students who could benefit from extra support with two proficient partners who act as models.

On Day Zero, you'll combine partnerships into study groups of four (or perhaps five for one or two groups). Students will often work with a partner, and occasionally with their whole study group. We've found that kids who are interested in the same topic often work well together, as their work is fueled by shared passion. You'll know your kids, so you can probably combine some partnerships strategically, thinking about who will work well together, who wants to work together, who will benefit from working together. You'll see that in Day Zero, partnerships put their names on Post-its® under topics they're interested in. That gives you the opportunity to do some rapid sorting and forming of study groups. Usually, if you say to students, "I've been thinking about you, and I think you could work really well together because . . . what do you think?" students will feel as if they've had a voice in their groupings.

Organizing Your Space

We think you'll find it helps your students if you establish separate, well-defined libraries in the classroom for each featured research topic. Whether you use bins, shelves, table tops, window sills, or a rolling cart, a well-defined library will keep each topic easily accessible for your study groups. Here is a tip: invite (or assign) a member of each study group to be the librarian for the resources for their group. The librarian can maintain the organization of the resources, incorporate new resources gathered by the study group, and monitor texts that are signed out overnight for continued research.

In addition, you will find it helpful to prepare your space to get ready for this unit of study. You will want to make sure unrelated charts from previous units are stored away, copies of notebook rubrics and checklists have been made, blank vocabulary cards for Bend I are ready, a chart for student partnerships is posted, access to mentor notebooks is available, and troubleshooting for any additional tech assistance that is needed for infographics at the end of Bend I and recording of TED talks and the end of Bend III is in place.

If you are lucky to have ample bulletin board or wall space in your room, you might want to consider assigning each research group their own board or, at least, a section of a board. Students can use the boards to communicate with other groups in other sections, keep track of homework plans, post images from their research, and be attuned to their topics in the outside world by posting connections to songs, books, film, communities, current events, and so on. In Bend III, these concept boards could be used as backdrops for TED talks.

Marking Up and Rehearsing the Read-Aloud

There are three read-alouds in the unit—one at the start of each bend. All of the texts relate to the teacher-demonstration research topic for the unit, which is freedom of speech. We chose this topic for the texts used in minilessons and read-aloud for the whole class, since no matter what topic a researcher cares about, knowledge of free speech will inform how one goes about informing and persuading others. Free speech is going to be relevant to ELA and social studies teachers, we know. If you are a science teacher, the first and third read-alouds are related to climate impact, in addition to free speech. We make a suggestion, below, for an alternate second read-aloud, of a text related to free speech and science.

The first read-aloud, in Session 1, is a video about teen activist, Xiuhtezcatl Tonatiuh. It's called "The Fifteen-Year-Old Suing the Government over Climate Change," and it's about how Xiuhtezcatl and his group of young activist companions raise their voices in activism, and use their knowledge of free speech to get their message across.

We strongly suggest downloading and previewing the video first, for a few reasons. One, if your situation is like ours, you can be sure that when you want to show it, the Internet won't work, and if it does work, YouTube will be blocked, and if those both work, something else will go wrong with your digital connection! But, the other reason we suggest you preview is that in the prologue, before the title page, Xiuhtezcatl uses some minor foul language. It's likely your students will have heard this word before, but we also want to give you the opportunity to start the video after this point, at the title credits. (There is a short National Geographic video on Xiuhtezcatl called, "Kid Warrior Fights Climate Change," as an alternate text.)

In this first read-aloud session, we've suggested lenses that will be helpful for readers to have in mind as they watch. These lenses engage students in reading for implicit as well as explicit ideas. What's most important is that students are prompted for these lenses before they watch the next session, so they are reading with this lens in mind. The video is engaging and accessible, but the level of thinking you'll ask students to do is very high. For this reason, if you teach an inclusion class or have students who are language learners, you may want to preview the video with these students beforehand, so they are watching it for the second time during the read-aloud.

The second read-aloud, which launches Bend II, is a *New York Times* article, "High School Tells Student to Remove Anti-War Shirt." The article is about a high school student who tested the boundaries of free speech by wearing a shirt to school that was a political critique. Again, you'll see that we suggest a series of lenses that you'll prompt students to consider, before reading each section. These lenses aim to help students tease out the disputes and arguments inside of a topic, including which groups or voices represent various perspectives. This article will be one that you may also want to preview with language learners and students who may benefit from extra support with the text. Reading it more than once will also be a good support.

If you are a science teacher, we suggest this text as an alternate: "The Scientific Importance of Free Speech," by Adam Perkins, published in *Quillette* (https://quillette.com/2018/04/13/scientific-importance-free-speech/). It's in the Freedom of Speech text set. It is a fascinating look at how scientists sometimes deliberately squash other scientists' findings.

The third read-aloud launches Bend III. In this read-aloud session you'll show two videos, "Our Campaign to Ban Plastic Bags in Bali," a TED talk presented by teens Melati and Isabel Wijsen, and a TED talk, "Hackschooling Makes Me Happy," presented by Logan LaPlante. Both these texts show teens using their research and their knowledge of free speech to create change. This read-aloud session will be an inquiry into the qualities of TED talks as a form of activist social media—their purpose, their structure, their craft. You won't need to watch the entirety of both these talks. We suggest that you watch about five to seven minutes of each, so that you have time to reread parts, and study groups then have time to go think about their own talks. (The talks are each about eleven minutes long.)

Preparing Your Own Research Notebook

Across the unit of study, students will take their notes and notebook work seriously. They'll begin with lean note-taking. They'll incorporate vocabulary acquisition. They'll learn to create synthesis pages and infographics. They'll move to deeper note-taking and a study of mentor notebooks.

We've provided an array of mentor notebook pages to inspire students. Your own notebook will also model for students how a researcher moves from lean notes to deeper notes. Your notebook doesn't have to be real—it can be a pure demonstration text, in which you demonstrate how you do some jotting during the read-aloud, and you share some sample pages where you've kept track of sources, created some synthesis pages, and so on. It's really helpful for students if you have samples of these kinds of pages in your demonstration notebook:

- Lean notes—the kind you take when you are building background knowledge and reading fast and furiously

- Vocabulary acquisition—a system for collecting vocabulary which you can then sort conceptually

- Synthesis pages—where you consolidate your knowledge, often with diagrams or infographics

- Annotation—where you go back into your notes to add new thinking, make connections, pose questions

- Long writing—where you reflect on how your thinking has changed

- Deeper notes—where you are working toward a project, in this case, doing ethical research on sides of an argument

- Sources—we suggest a continuum, which helps you keep track of sources and assess the fairness of your research

- Mentor text studies—jottings that show the influence of a mentor text

In the online resources, we've provided myriad student samples of these kinds of pages.

Preview the Pacing of the Sessions

This unit, like all our units of study, is fast-paced and intense. It's a terrific four- to six-week unit. It's not necessarily a terrific eight- to twelve-week unit. The goal is to teach kids to build background knowledge quickly, and then to research with a narrower focus on an argument inside a topic, and then to come to an informed position. So one goal of this work is to teach kids to work with intensity. All of these topics are fascinating for a few weeks, and this intellectual work is fascinating for a few weeks at a time.

We piloted these sessions especially in Marc's classroom, where he has forty-two-minute periods. There are twenty-one sessions. There are, though, two sessions where we imagine you may want to consider giving kids an extra work period. Those include the session on creating infographics (Session 7), and the session on preparing TED talks (Session 19).

If you decide to stretch the unit, you may want to have study groups shift to a new topic before Bend III, and then rapidly duplicate the work of Bend I, focusing on the research rather than the lessons on how to function in a study group, and letting kids take charge of their research using their experience from Bend II, before going on to TED talks.

If you need to shorten the unit, you could end at flash-debates, and leave TED talks for another time. If you do that, you may want to make a bigger deal of the flash-debates, perhaps setting up a schedule so that each study group has an audience for their debate.

ONLINE DIGITAL RESOURCES

A variety of resources to accompany this unit of study are available in the online resources, including charts and examples of student work shown throughout *Essential Research Skills for Teens*, as well as links to other electronic resources. Offering daily support for your teaching, these materials will help you provide a structured learning environment that fosters independence and self-direction.

To access and download all the digital resources for *Essential Research Skills for Teens*:

1. Go to www.heinemann.com and click the link in the upper right to log in. (If you do not have an account yet, you will need to create one.)

2. Enter the following registration code in the box to register your product: MSRUOS_MATF7

3. Enter the security information requested.

4. Once you have registered your product, it will appear in the list of My Online Resources.

(You may keep copies of these resources on up to six of your own computers or devices. By downloading the files, you acknowledge that they are for your individual or classroom use and that neither the resources nor the product code will be distributed or shared.)

A Letter to Teachers

Dear Colleagues,

The goal of this bend is to instill study habits that will help your students to be highly successful in high school and college. That includes teaching students to build their own background knowledge, to collect and revisit notes, and to be able to work as a study partner in collaborative groups. We want all of your students to develop the social and academic capital that lets young people move with confidence through their academic and professional endeavors.

BUILDING BACKGROUND KNOWLEDGE

One of the things that most leads to academic success is background knowledge. Quite simply, kids who know more do better in science and history classes. They come to class with a sense of context, and with familiarity with some concepts and vocabulary, so that when they encounter the same new learning as other students, they are less daunted by it. They have points of familiarity to ground their new learning. We want to offer this for all kids as a skill set that will empower them. We want all students to know that in any class, or any pursuit, they can set out to build their own background knowledge quickly.

To that end, one big thing you'll be teaching your kids in this bend is the art of building background knowledge by immersing themselves quickly in accessible texts. In this early immersion you'll lead kids away from taking tons of detailed notes (which they may want to do), or from closely reading one or two pages in a class period. Instead, you'll teach your kids that when building background knowledge, they need to take in information fast and furiously, which means watching videos, reading accessible books and articles, and mostly, getting the lay of the land of this new topic.

You'll start students with some curated text sets. We offer a range of sets on historical topics, science topics, and civics to help students get started, and of course, you are welcome to curate your own. We chose to begin with curated sets rather than to set students to conducting their own open research, as the aim of this bend is for kids to understand what it feels like to read a lot on a topic, quickly. In Bend II, you will support students conducting more research from scratch, teaching critical literacy skills regarding the Internet to facilitate this.

NOTE-TAKING, NOTEBOOKS, AND INFOGRAPHICS

You'll start your students in research notebooks, and you will teach them to take lean notes while reading. They will be doing quite a bit of sketching and flowcharting, which is why we suggest paper rather than digital notebooks. There has also been some interesting research on how different parts of the brain are mobilized when working by hand that suggests that giving up sketch notebooks entirely may be a mistake. Tablets can also work well for kids who work more rapidly on digital devices (tablets let kids sketch as well as take other kinds of notes). These notes are lean so that kids spend most of their time reading. They'll use talk to process a lot of what they learn.

Our informal studies of successful high school students in the high schools we work with suggest that kids who do well academically often go back into their notes a lot more than other students. They make study guides and summaries, they reorganize, they categorize, they annotate. You'll share this research with students, and you'll give students an entire period, or possibly two if you think they'll need more time, to consider what they've learned so far and go back into their notebooks to create synthesis pages.

After students have synthesized their learning, you'll move them toward working on infographics that help them collect their growing knowledge inside of the topic. Moving from lean notes to synthesis to more complex visualization will help kids think about what's important as they build deeper background knowledge. You'll see that we suggest taking the time to introduce kids to software such as Piktochart, Venngage, or Canva. When kids have to think about what template to use, and how to organize information, as well as what to include in different parts, it forces them to think about their information. One note: It may be helpful if you find out which of your students are digitally adept, and ask them to pilot this software ahead of time, so they can help coach other students. You may also want to ask your school to purchase the software, so kids have more choices of templates and tools than those available for free.

BECOMING EFFECTIVE STUDY PARTNERS

There is one more big goal of this bend, and that is to coach kids in becoming a strong study partner and working effectively in a study group. From our own high school research, and that of Tony Wagner (*The Global Achievement Gap*), and Paul Tough (*How Children Succeed*), we know that kids who become adept at studying with others find those skills stand them in good stead when they take challenging academic classes. But not all kids are equally adept at being study partners, for all sorts of reasons. You'll see, then, that you'll engage your students in studying Susan Cain's work with teen introverts (*Quiet Power*), and Gladwell's work with social intelligence (*Outliers*), so that they come to better know themselves as students, and learn to harness their strengths for their own studies and in collaborative study groups.

RESEARCHING KIDS' STUDY HABITS, QUIRKS, AND POTENTIAL STRENGTHS

As all of this essential foundational work unrolls, as the kids are beginning to research their topics, you'll be researching them. You're figuring out what study habits your students already have, and what they can build on. You'll coach students to begin to have agency over their own study habits. You'll be transparent about what it means to build background knowledge, to work collaboratively with a small team of peers, to do quick and meaningful homework. You'll help kids do some essential, fast, and light note-taking; you'll work on their talk skills; and you'll set them up to better understand themselves as learners. Both you and your kids will need a "meta" approach to the work, as ultimately, you both care that they learn *content*, and you care that they learn *how to access content*. The kids will finalize the work of this bend by teaching another study group much of what they've learned using visuals and notes to explain some of the most important aspects of their research so far.

HARNESSING A SHARED CLASS TOPIC FOR READ-ALOUD AND MINILESSONS

As the kids work in study groups using curated text sets, you'll demonstrate in your minilessons and read-aloud by diving into research on a demonstration topic. We suggest the topic of free speech. We chose this topic because it spans civics, history, and science. All activists and all researchers need to know something about free speech if they hope to influence others. Understanding more about the history of free speech in the nation in which you live, as well as the challenges to free speech in places around the world, is crucial to coming of age as a researcher. We live in a nation in which the boundaries of free speech call into question all sorts of ethical as well as legal issues. We live in an age in which ideas and information travel exponentially across media, faster than fact checking. It's exhilarating and horrifying, and it would be good if our students, future voters all, grappled with the complicated ethics of free speech.

All the best,
Mary and Marc

Day Zero—Forming Research Clubs and Choosing Research Topics

GETTING READY

✔ Make sure your partnerships are established, so that students are previewing research topics by partnership (see Connection).

✔ Prepare to show a video clip of Katniss's speech to President Snow from the film *Mockingjay*, of the Hunger Games trilogy. A link to this clip is available in the online resources (see Teaching).

✔ Create a list of possible research topics for students to preview (see Active Engagement).

✔ Provide students with access to the starter text sets (see Link).

IN THIS SESSION

TODAY you'll teach students that researchers choose topics they find engaging, and they find others to work with who share their interests.

TODAY YOUR STUDENTS will work with a partner to browse text sets, talking with each other, and then will work with another partnership to form a study group around a shared research topic. You'll facilitate this process.

MINILESSON

CONNECTION

Give a little keynote to stir students up to embark on significant new work—research work that will empower them. Remind students of initial habits, as well.

"We are getting ready to start a new unit of study today. Here's what you'll be embarking on. You'll be learning how to conduct research where not only do you build knowledge, but you also use that knowledge to take up stances. The unit will culminate in you all giving teen TED talks."

Invite students to share moments when they have wished things were different, when something seemed unfair or unjust.

"To get ready for this work, will you take a moment and think about any moment when you felt like something wasn't right, something wasn't fair, and you wished you knew enough or were powerful enough to change things? It could be a moment in history, in the world, or in your life. Think for a moment, and when you have an idea, turn and explain it to your partner."

The room erupted with conversations about issues ranging from curfews and cellphone use, to animal rights, to greenhouse gases, to gender equity and racial bias.

❖ **Name the teaching point.**

"Researchers, today I want to teach you that when you tackle activist research, you commit not only to reading deeply on a topic, but to the possibility of being changed by your research, and to changing others as well. That means you want to choose topics you find fascinating and relevant to things you care about in the world."

TEACHING

Invite students to share a topic you care deeply about—in this example, free speech—by thinking about how you see it around you in popular culture, such as a scene from _Mockingjay_.

"Let me show you what I mean. I've become interested in the question of free speech—the risks people take around the world to speak out, and the effect speech can have as a catalyst for change. One way I know that I am truly fascinated by this issue is that I feel like I see it everywhere—I not only see obvious references to it in the news, I also see the issue hiding in stories.

"For instance, think alongside me for a moment. I want to revisit a moment from _Mockingjay_, part three of The Hunger Games trilogy. It's the moment when Katniss is with the rebels, fighting against President Snow, and she visits District 8. President Snow's forces have just bombed a hospital full of children and wounded soldiers.

"Will you watch, and as you watch, will you ask: How does the impact of free speech play out in this moment?" I played the clip, Katniss's speech to President Snow, and invited partners to share their thinking.

Summarize some of what students say, and use the engagement with Katniss and free speech as a segue to students finding topics they care deeply about and see in the world around them.

I listened as students talked, collected a few examples to share, and called them together to summarize. "I heard you talk about how Katniss is talking not only to President Snow, but also to her fellow resistance fighters—to those who are already fighting, and those she wants to stir up to fight.

"It's inspiring, even though Katniss is a fictional character. Here's why, I think; it's because Katniss is aware of the power of speech and she is using that power to its fullest capacity.

"This fictional moment makes me think about other moments when people have been able to stir up others with their words, as well as other moments when people have been silenced. I think, no matter what topic you get fired up about, knowing more about free speech will be relevant because it relates to how you speak up about the topic.

Even older students love to gather in a meeting area—as if they are huddling with a coach. You'll get a tremendous increase in intensity in settings like these.

"Researchers, do you see how I've found a topic that I think is so interesting that I see its impact all around me? I can imagine reading more about it, I'm interested in its history and its current relevance, and I'm dying to read and talk about it with others. That's what you want when you choose a topic to research. You want to choose something that feels important to you, something that you see as significant in the world around you, whether it's in news events or fiction or film or history."

ACTIVE ENGAGEMENT

Invite students to talk for a few minutes about topics they already care about or have some experience with, using the text sets you've created as preliminary topic choices.

"Researchers, you're looking for a topic that you can imagine being deeply engaged in, not just in school, but in a way that positions you and your friends as potential activists. Will you take a moment to think about some of these topics, and then talk with your partner about any of them that seem especially important?" I displayed our list of research possibilities.

Historical Topics	Contemporary Civics Issues	Science Studies
• Immigration	• Immigration Bias	• Plastics Pollution
• Free Speech	• Racial Bias	• Ecosystem Preservation
• Voting Rights	• Gun Violence	• Fishing Rights
• Segregation	• War on Drugs	• Green Energy Choices
• Gun Control	• Gender and Sexual Identity	• Water Rights
• Rights of Indigenous Peoples	Equity	• Climate Change
	• Climate Change	

Soon partners were talking about which issues they were familiar with, from school or current events or in their lives. I listened for evidence of real interest.

Share with students how you can hear when a topic seems particularly interesting—and add that it's the sense of excitement and curiosity that fuels powerful research.

"Researchers, as I listen to you, I can hear when a topic has real potential for you as an activist research topic. I can hear it when your voice seems excited, when you seem especially curious, and sometimes, when you express outrage. For some of you, it's because you've read books or seen films about this issue. For others, it's because you've seen it in the news. And for some of these topics, you've seen them play out in your lives or the lives of your friends and families. And maybe there is a topic here that you don't know a lot about, but you're curious about.

"The main thing is you've already begun to think about your interests and concerns. That's the most important first step in this work—to bring out your passions and let those shape your research choices. Let's give you time now, with your partner, to browse the text sets that will let you dive into these topics, and to come to a considered decision about what it is that you want to research. Then, we'll work to combine partnerships, so that you'll have a research club."

Teachers, we've provided text sets for research topics in three areas: historical topics, contemporary civics issues, and science studies. Depending on the subject you teach, you might offer one of these sets of research topics, or provide a mix of topics and text sets. Young researchers benefit hugely from curated text sets to launch their research. They can add to these text sets as they move farther into research. If a research group wants to pursue a topic you haven't offered, we suggest the students put together a preliminary text set (which you may help them with) as evidence of viability.

LINK

Set partnerships up to browse the available text sets and come to a shared decision about their research topic. Give a tip about how to get started with some shared decision making.

"Researchers, today you are going to choose from among a few research topics, and the way you'll do that is by browsing text sets. I recommend that you read some snippets of texts, and then perhaps preview a different text set. When you find a topic that interests you, put your partnership names on a Post-it, and put that Post-it under the topic on this chart paper. It's fine if you put your names under a few topics—that will help us form study groups more easily.

"The goal today is to form study groups, and you'll do this by pairing up with another partnership to make a group of four, or five if your partnership has three people, and you want to study with others who care about the same topic. You might not even know that there are other kids in here who share some of your interests. Let's find that out now.

"As you go off to do this work, remember to pay attention to how a topic stirs you. Think about where you've seen this issue before, think about why you care about it. Ask yourself what you're curious about. All of that questioning will help you choose a research topic that you can do serious work with and that has the potential to change you. By the end of this period, you'll hopefully know both your topic, and who else will be researching that with you. I'll help facilitate all of this. Your goal is to figure out what you're interested in."

Padlets make it easier for students to access digital texts on any device.

It's important to have books and articles.

Negotiating Partnerships into Shared Research Topics and Study Groups

BY THE END OF THIS CONFERRING TIME, you'll need to have helped partnerships join with another partnership to form a study group that has committed to a shared research topic. We've done this, and it takes just a little finesse. This is a great opportunity for kids who have shared interests to go far with their research. In general, we find that interest in a topic trumps other concerns such as reading level or past academic histories. Kids surprise us when they care.

Here's what we've done during this time: we help partnerships begin to put their names under some topics pretty quickly—that is, when partnerships feel like they're interested in a topic, say, "Oh, great, let's write your name down there, and why don't you check out another topic, now?" Clearly, if a few partnerships are interested in a few topics, you have more flexibility as you help organize kids into groups.

One place you may run into trouble is if you have a partnership that is stuck on one particular topic, and no one else wants that. A study group isn't going to go well with just two people, as there is a lot of shared work in this unit—and if someone is absent, that partner has nobody to work with. So you may need to do a little negotiation to shift another partnership into or out of a topic. Usually saying "I was thinking about you when I looked at this research topic—come see" may help get kids into a topic.

By the end of work time, your goal as a teacher is to move from having twelve to sixteen partnerships in the class to having six to eight study groups, of four to five kids each. So you're helping kids put their names up under topics, then doing some matching, using your teacher finesse to combine partnerships in ways that make kids excited and you hopeful.

Here are some tips that may help with this work.

If you notice . . .	Then you might . . .
Students are curious about everything and do not want to limit their choice but keep flitting from topic to topic, and you need them to commit, perhaps even commit to a topic where you need their partnership . . .	Remind students that all these text sets will be rewarding, all these topics are significant, and it really doesn't matter which topic they choose—they just need to choose something. You might suggest that they consider, in the lives that they live, in the time and place where they live, if any one topic is important in their lives. You might say, "I'm thinking about you, Diego, and how you always recycle your bottles and cans, and it feels like you already care about climate change," or "Sarah, I know you're a big hiker, you probably really care about the earth, and preserving it." Soon you can lead kids into a topic the same way you can lead them into a book, by making them feel like they have a personal interest in the topic.

If you notice . . .	Then you might . . .
Students seem distracted or slow to engage in any particular topic . . .	Give a kind of "topic introduction," like a trailer to a movie or an introduction to a book. "Researchers, I was thinking about you, and I wanted to show you a couple of the texts in this set, because they seemed like they would really interest you." Pull up an engaging video or article, and either read a bit aloud, or suggest they watch or read for a few minutes. Go visit another group, then come back and say something like, "What did you think? Wasn't it interesting how . . . ?" and act simply as a tremendously interested partner in this work. Often, playing a proficient partner as you study engaging texts is a way to move students toward focused, engaged work.
Students do not seem to feel a connection with any topic . . .	Invite students to think about the kind of work they may want to do in the future. Saying to them "I've often imagined that you'll be doing important work on civil liberties, or human rights, or protecting the planet" gives kids a vision of possible academic and professional identities. Alfred Tatum (*Reading for Their Life*) and Pedro Noguera (*City Schools and the American Dream*) both talk about the significance of role-playing kids into the academic identities you want for them. Look over the text sets, and think about how you might talk about possibility to certain kids in ways that help them see themselves as significant. You might say, "I see you taking up issues of gender already in your writing," or "I notice you standing up for people, in class and outside, and maybe one of these issues of human rights might be right for your group. Your research might help you think about work you want to do in the world, now or when you're older."
Students are hesitant to form a study group with another partnership . . . *see this as being a major roadblock for some*	Reintroduce them quickly as caring colleagues by highlighting their past academic, creative, and collaborative achievements. Chances are these students are hesitant because they do not know each other well or have misconceptions due to other classes or experiences. "What the four of you are about to discover is that research brings unique individuals together in the pursuit of understanding something greater than themselves." It might sound something like, "What you don't know about Cai Yi is that she is incredibly organized, which will be a huge asset to study your group" or "Jerson's strength is that he provides a valued perspective to any topic he studies, which will deepen your understanding." Peter Johnston (*Opening Minds*) reminds us to focus on collaborative strengths to ensure social and societal growth. Even addressing a concern can be framed in a collaborative mindset by saying, "Jack is working on staying on topic while researching in small groups. All of you will be a good influence on him by making sure you have a clear work plan before you get started."

Study Groups Work Together to Develop Research Plans

Invite students to sit with their research groups in the meeting area. Suggest they set their own homework, making a plan to preview their text sets so they are ready to launch tomorrow's work.

"Researchers, look up here at our chart, find your study group, and move quickly to sit with them." I waited a moment. "Take a moment to tell your group—what did you find fascinating about this topic? What brings you to this research group?"

After a couple of minutes, I interrupted. "It's great to see how a shared interest can bring together researchers like this. I want to give you a tip as you get ready to launch into this work. Tomorrow, you'll be diving into initial research. To do that, it will be helpful if you've previewed your text set, getting the lay of the land for what's available.

"Will you set your own homework now, with your study group? How will you access your research text set online outside of class? The URL for all the padlets is listed on the whiteboard, and you can pull that up on your phone, device, or any computer. Maybe jot it down so you can access it later.

"Talk to each other for a moment—how will you preview some of the texts? You don't have to start researching tonight, but when you have time to research tomorrow, you want to have a plan so you can dive right in."

Jaclyn supports her students with engaging small versions of tools and charts that act as reminders.

DAY ZERO HOMEWORK

 ## PREVIEWING TEXT SETS TO PREPARE FOR RESEARCH

Tonight, take ten minutes or so to preview your text set, so that you know what text you want to begin with when you start researching tomorrow. You might open a few texts, see which texts feel easier to get started with, and mostly, have a plan so that you can dive in quickly tomorrow.

Read-Aloud

*Discerning Explicit and Implicit Ideas
in Complex Nonfiction*

IN THIS SESSION

TODAY you'll teach students that when beginning a study of a new topic, researchers build their background knowledge by quickly reading more accessible texts. As they read these texts, they work on pulling out both explicit and implicit ideas. You'll demonstrate this work with a read-aloud.

TODAY YOUR STUDENTS will first engage in inferring in reading with a shared read-aloud. Then, they will work with a partner to begin building their background knowledge on the topic they've chosen in their research groups. They'll decide which texts to read, and begin reading. At the end of this session, students will set homework goals. Study groups do not meet today.

GETTING READY

✔ Provision students with research notebooks, and have ready your own demonstration research notebook.

✔ Research partners should sit together at the meeting area (see Connection).

✔ Be prepared to display a visual of a padlet with the titles and descriptions for the class to see, or prepare a short annotated bibliography to share (see Connection).

✔ You'll show a video about Xiuhtezcatl Tonatiuh, a fifteen-year-old environmental activist who sued the government over climate change.

✔ Prepare to begin an anchor chart, "When immersing oneself in a topic, researchers . . ." (see Link).

✔ Provision students with initial starter text sets (see Link).

CONNECTION

Introduce the big work of the unit, which is to increase students' powers as researchers. Invite kids to imagine times in the future when those skills could be useful.

"Researchers, we're starting a new unit of study today. Let's talk about some of the goals of this unit. The whole aim of this unit is for you to become a more powerful researcher, someone who can dive into any topic, even a totally unfamiliar one, and find out a lot, rapidly. That kind of intense learning will eventually let you take an educated, powerful position, one that lets you argue, debate, and bring others to stances that you think matter.

"Just for a moment, will you think of any situation that might come up, in the next five to ten years, when it would be helpful to be skilled at this kind of rapid research? Think about scenarios outside of school as well as classes. When you have an idea, tell your partner."

Listen in as kids talk, so you can name some of their ideas.

"I heard some of you talk about researching to get a job—that's so wise, to do some research *before* an interview. Some of you talked about research projects that you might do in science and history classes. Some of you imagined the kinds of jobs where you have to research new markets, new places, or people and communities. Some of you thought about activist work—how you might want to advocate and persuade others to take up positions you care a lot about.

"Here's the thing—if you become skilled at research, you'll use those skills the rest of your life. Which brings us to the questions: How do you start? What skills matter most?"

Tell students about the significance of building background knowledge and learning to work in study groups.

"It turns out there is a bunch of research on this. When researchers study kids who do very well in high school and college, these kids often display some of the same essential skills. One skill is being able to speak in compelling ways, using research to support your ideas. You'll be doing that work later in this unit. But there is a skill set that comes before that. To defend positions from an informed stance you have to know a lot. And it turns out that some kids come to class, or to any new experience, already *knowing more*. These students know how to prepare—how to build their own background knowledge. If they take a class and it turns out they don't know much about the topic, they find out more. Not only that, often they figure out what their class will be studying, and they do a little work ahead of time.

"I think the best comparison here is to think about kids getting ready for soccer season. Kids who want to play, who want to start, don't wait for the first practice. Instead, they kick the ball around ahead of time. They train on their own. They increase their readiness.

"So that's what I want to help you with over this first part of this research unit. I want to help you become skilled at building your own background knowledge. So, you'll both learn a lot about the topic you've chosen, and you'll become a more powerful researcher."

Remind students that to begin building background knowledge, they should start with more accessible and interesting texts and read a lot, quickly. Then set kids up to begin today's read-aloud text.

"Researchers, there are two things to know about this work. One, when you are building background knowledge, there is no text that is too easy. And second, you want to read as much as possible, as quickly as possible. So, rather than getting dragged into a hard text, or into lots of detailed note-taking, you're reading to get the lay of the land—quickly. It's a sort of rapid reading, where you're not getting stuck on tricky details or hard parts yet, but instead you read, summarize the text so far, read more, and so on.

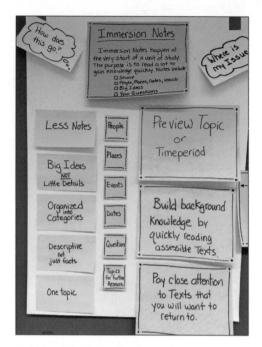

FIG. 1–1   You'll need to coach students to spend most of their time reading, and to take lean notes when reading, to build background knowledge.

"Let me show you what I mean. I'm researching free speech, so you can learn alongside me. First, we need to choose a text." I showed students the free speech text set, including articles, videos, and infographics.

"Look over these titles and descriptions for a moment. Then think with your partner—where do you recommend we begin, and why? What text might we start with?"

I gave students a moment to look over titles and descriptions and to talk with a partner.

Shift to introducing the text that you'll read aloud and the work that you'll begin today, of summarizing texts as you read.

"Researchers, I hear you suggesting that we start with a text that feels easier, or that feels like it may give more background, more context. A couple of you suggested that starting with something that seems especially engaging might be a great way to lead into the topic. That makes a lot of sense. Many of you were intrigued by this video, 'The Fifteen-Year-Old Environmental Activist Suing the Government over Climate Change.' It's published by *Vice Magazine*, which does a lot of fantastic digital journalism. Let's read that one."

Shift to introducing the work of the bend, and today's teaching, that readers need to look for implicit as well as explicit ideas in texts.

"Researchers, when you're researching a topic, the texts you read may or may not explicitly be about your topic right from the start. It may take a bit for the text to get to your topic. Or there may be ideas hidden in the text that address your topic in implicit ways. That means that readers need to consider how parts of the text relate to their topic, both explicitly and implicitly—in obvious ways and more subtle ways."

CONDUCTING THE READ-ALOUD

Engage students in watching the first part of your digital text. Remind them that the text may or may not explicitly say anything about free speech.

"Let's try that out. Let's read—watch—the first part of this digital text. Will you get ready to share with a partner what seems most important here so far, and any ways this text is related to issues of free speech? Again, remember that it may or may not *explicitly* say anything about free speech."

I showed the first minute of "The Fifteen-Year-Old Environmental Activist Suing the Government over Climate Change" (just Xiuhtezcatl introducing himself and his cause) and then invited partners to talk.

Teachers, if your students have come of age in Units of Study, *then they've learned to preview text sets and make smart choices about beginning with more accessible and more engaging texts. They would have practiced this work explicitly in* Tapping the Power of Nonfiction, *and they would have also practiced it in* Historical Fiction Book Clubs. *But we still see kids, all too often, pick up the first text that came to hand without evaluating it. It may be the influence of too many classes where kids had little opportunity to make choices about their reading. We're not sure, but we do find it's important to remind kids to preview texts and make smart nonfiction reading plans.*

Teachers, you can start the video at thirty seconds, right when it rolls the credits with the words Climate Changer, *and that way you can skip our young activist saying a bad word in the prologue. Part of what we explore in free speech is what teens are allowed to say and not say, and this is a very minor bad word! But still, you know your classroom norms, so decide where to start.*

After listening to students for a moment, call them back and summarize a bit of what they learned from the text so far, reminding students of the power of rereading and of talking about new learning with a study partner.

"So fascinating! So, Xiuhtezcatl is a fifteen-year-old, and he sued the United States government! And Xiuhtez-catl describes himself as a climate warrior. So, let's see, if we were to try to capture an explicit idea here, I guess it's that teens can sue the U.S. government. And is there anything implicit—any other way this text relates to the topic of free speech? Let's reread for a moment; powerful readers reread on the run all the time."

I rewound the text for a moment to Xiuhtezcatl introducing himself, and we watched that bit again.

"Well, now that I hear this again, I have some new thinking. Give a nod or a thumbs up if this matches some of your thinking. I guess I'm thinking that this teen has found multiple ways to raise his voice. He sued the government, he gives interviews, and he calls himself a 'climate warrior.' So, it feels to me like one idea that is hiding in this text is that some teens are using their free speech rights to assert their ideas.

"Readers, it's especially helpful to both reread on the run, and to talk with a thought partner or study partner when you are studying something new, so that together, you can figure out what's most important, including ideas that are hiding in the text."

Restate how you looked for ideas that are hiding in the text, as well as ones that are explicit. Then invite students to try this thinking out as they keep reading.

"Readers, what matters here is that we tried to summarize what the text said explicitly—that teens sued the U.S. government, *and* we thought about ideas that are hiding in the text, like how the actions Xiuhtezcatl takes show that teens can use the power of free speech to assert their ideas.

"Let's read on, and will you and your partner keep doing this work? Try to pull out what this text teaches you on the surface, and also what's hidden, or below the surface—it's like you have to read between the lines."

I rewound, and played about another two minutes of the video, of Xiuhtezcatl as a very young boy, giving speeches and organizing marches. Then I invited students to talk with a partner.

"What are you learning here, readers? What seems most important?"

Restate some of the central ideas and then give another tip before reading on—that researchers take lean notes as they read.

"Wow, this kid has engaged in some significant activism! So, in terms of what you are learning, some of you said that one idea that feels central so far is that some kids become activists even when they are very young.

Teachers, you'll notice that we are using the term study partner, *rather than simply* partner. *That's because we are working to conceptualize partnerships as something that can happen outside of school. We know that kids who can get and be study partners often do better in school—and we are trying to equalize this opportunity by role-playing kids into this work.*

Teachers, listen to students, trying to get a rapid idea of the range of idea building in the class. Kids' responses will range, depending on their experience with summarizing nonfiction, their skills at interpreting implicit ideas, their familiarity with the topic, and how accessible they find the text. Listen for ideas that can serve as examples, listen for kids whom you can quote (or with a little help, elevate), and note kids who may need support.

Xiuhtezcatl was giving speeches when he was six. And then, this is much more implicit, but some of you noted that free speech not only seems to protect people's right to speak up against the government, it seems to protect even kids' rights.

"Researchers, when you're reading, you have to figure out whether to read the whole text once, and then go back and jot some notes as you reread, or if you want to pause as you read, and jot some very quick notes. The main thing is to not slow down your reading—and often, your urge will be to take too many notes, too quickly, before you know what's important.

"Let me show you how I might take some extremely lean notes, ones that won't slow down my reading. I'd probably use something simple like boxes and bullets. In the box, I'd jot an idea that I think might be emerging as important, then I'd aim to collect quick details that fit with that idea.

"So, let's see, thinking back about what we've learned so far, if I were taking some lean notes in my notebook, they might look like this . . ." I placed my demonstration notebook under the document camera, and jotted:

> **Title: 'The Fifteen-Year-Old Environmental Activist**
> **Suing the Government over Climate Change'**
>
> <u>Vice</u>
>
> | Kids use free speech to assert their ideas |
> | --- |
>
> • Xiuhtezcatl gave speeches about protecting the environ-
>   ment when he was 6.

"Do you see how I didn't try to capture every bit of information, but instead, I summarized a big idea—in this case, one that is kind of implicit. The text is *explicitly* about Xiuhtezcatl. But it's *implicitly* about how kids like him use free speech, which is what I'm researching. But readers, as you read, don't be bound just by your idea of your topic. As we keep reading, we may learn more about free speech. But we may learn other stuff, too, and we want to be open to new ideas."

Colleen Cruz, author of Writers Read Better: Nonfiction, *teaches that there are two reading strategies that vastly increase comprehension. For fiction, it's rereading. For nonfiction, it's previewing. You can do some of both here—previewing the very beginning and rereading along the way.*

Read on, inviting students to continue the work of reading between the lines, inferring implicit ideas as well as explicit. Let them know that for longer, denser texts, they'll have to summarize parts of the text, and invite them to take some agency over when to pause and talk.

"Readers, often the texts you'll read will have lots of information, and you don't want to pause at every paragraph, or every twenty seconds. Instead, read long parts, and then pause to make sense of those parts. Let's read on, and give me a signal when you've learned enough that you think that is worth talking to your partner."

I rewound back to 1:00, so that kids could reread, and then I continued the text, stopping, at kids' signals, after Xiuhtezcatl describes how they got communities to ban fracking, and he says, "more to come" (around 5:46).

I gave students a minute to talk.

Summarize again, noting that readers need to follow the ideas of the text, not make the text follow their ideas. Then suggest that kids do some rapid, lean jotting, and model how you would continue to take lean notes.

"Readers, it's so interesting listening to you. A lot of you were interested in how some of the care Xiuhtez-catl has for the environment came with his identity as Aztec. Some of you were fascinated by how much he knows about fracking, and environmental damage. And pretty much all of us were impressed by how much he accomplished—how Xiuhtezcatl and his team of kid activists got his local communities to ban fracking.

"What's super important here is that you didn't try to force the text to fit our first ideas about free speech—you didn't just look for evidence that kids use free speech to assert their ideas. You also followed the text, learning other ideas that were unexpected."

I suggested that kids do some jotting, and I opened my demonstration notebook, to model some lean note-taking. "So, let's take some lean notes, and see how they compare." I jotted.

> Kids use free speech to assert their ideas
>
> • Xiuhtezcatl gave speeches about protecting the environ-
>   ment when he was 6.
> • Xiuhtezcatl and his friends started an activist group and
>   organized marches and protests.

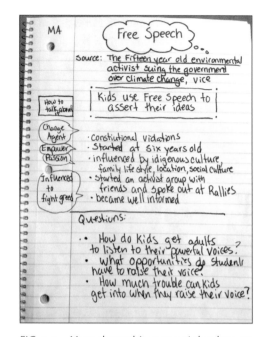

FIG. 1–2   Marc shares his own notebook as an implicit demonstration during the read-aloud.

Give students a moment to compare what they jotted. Then note that not all notes will fit in one structure, and encourage students to take notes in other ways as well, as the text and their thinking suggest.

"Go ahead, readers, compare what you jotted with a partner." I waited a moment.

"Readers, sometimes you'll feel like some of your thinking and questions don't fit inside of boxes and bullets. You might find that you want to jot a flowchart, or make a diagram, or something else. For example, I have some questions now, so I think I'll *list* the questions that are coming up for me around some of these ideas. Maybe I'll put a box around those, or write them in a different color." I jotted.

> Questions
>
> • Do kids get in trouble for civil disobedience—like Xiuhtezcatl and his friends taking over the county meeting?
> • How did Xiuhtezcatl and his friends get adults to listen to them so seriously?

You can use your own notebook to demonstrate flexibility in note-taking structures, matching your structure to your purpose.

Finish the read-aloud, inviting students to consider if there are any other points they want to talk about and add to their notes, and other questions or new thinking they want to capture.

"Let's finish the text and see what else you are struck by, what else you might add to talk about with your partner, and possibly add to your notes."

I played the rest of the video. There were murmurs at the end, and I gave students an opportunity to talk with their partners while I listened in.

"Readers, this topic is troubling, and this kid is impressive. I think the biggest thing I'm coming away with is how important it is for kids to understand their right to free speech, and how to assert that right. Xiuhtezcatl and his friends aren't setting out to please. They are setting out to be heard."

LINK

Recap the work you did, reminding students that when reading complex and well-written or well-produced nonfiction, readers need to think about the ideas that are suggested, to read between the lines.

"Readers, let's send you off to work so you can get started with the topic your study group chose. Let's recap the steps you'll want to follow—not just today, but whenever you're building background knowledge.

"First, you want to make a smart choice about text, choosing something accessible so you can get a lot of reading done—and that could also include listening or watching. Second, make a reading plan, not just for yourself but with your study partner. Either choose the same text, and pause every now and then to talk, or arrange to teach each other about the texts you read on your own. Lastly, don't expect the text to stay solely on your idea of your topic—expect to think about what you're reading, and to figure out ideas that are hiding in the text. Finally, take some lean notes, to hold onto the big essentials and any questions.

"Today, you're reading to build background knowledge, and that means getting a lot of reading done quickly. Aim to get most of one text read, and take some lean notes. You can either finish for homework, or if you finish a text now, you can start a different text tonight. Choose an article, video, or website to explore."

I started the "When immersing oneself in a topic, researchers . . ." anchor chart.

ANCHOR CHART

When immersing oneself in a topic, researchers . . .

- **Build background knowledge rapidly by**
  - **Beginning with accessible and engaging texts**
  - **Reading thoughtfully, thinking about ideas that are hiding in the text**
  - **Pausing to note important ideas, information, and questions**

Build background knowledge rapidly

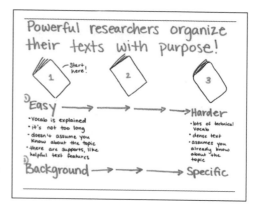

FIG. 1–3 Jaclyn's small versions of charts help her students make smart independent choices and get a lot of reading done.

Teachers, if it's possible to do some strategic book ordering, include books as well, as we know that when kids have access to accessible, engaging nonfiction books, they often read at much higher volume.

Supporting Students with Reading to Learn and Talking to Teach

You won't have a lot of time for conferring today, so it will help if you're prepared with some predictable conferences that may be appropriate today and across this week. Here are a few typical ways that kids may benefit from support, and some clues that they could use a little help.

Supporting Students with Reading to Learn and Talking to Teach	
If . . .	**Then you might . . .**
Students need support engaging with content, either because they struggle with reading or they struggle with engagement . . .	Preteach some content using a set of visual images. Talk with students a bit about some of these images, explain what some of them are, and use this as a way to introduce some content knowledge and to interest students in the topic.
Students begin to take copious notes almost as soon as they begin reading . . .	Intervene! Suggest that when they were younger, they used to chunk texts into smaller sections. But now the texts they are reading are longer, and they want to break them into much larger chunks. Help students make some decisions about bigger chunks of texts. Suggest, as well, that they *talk* through what seems important so far, rather than jotting every detail.
Students still insist on detailed note-taking, so that they are getting little reading done . . .	Suggest that they flag the text instead of taking notes at this stage, if it is a print text. Then they can return to these parts later, and decide after reading the whole text if there are a few things worth jotting at this point. If it's a digital text, suggest they put three Post-its in front of them, and they note the time frame when they think something important comes up. Then, they can return to jot, if needed, at the end.
Students struggle to summarize, giving long, rambling retellings with little coherence . . .	Try having students jot a boxes-and-bullets Post-it or two, where they box out one point the author makes, and then two or three supporting details. If some students still struggle, you can try playing the role of proficient partner, talking through some big ideas so these students are ready to share with a partner. You might need to investigate these kids' reading levels, and see if the texts are accessible for them.

FIG. 1–4 Sometimes simply listening to a student talk about what they find interesting can turn into an intimate conference where you help them intensify their interest in a topic.

SHARE

Compliment students on the way they began building background knowledge. Then encourage them to prepare for partner talk by taking time to think about what they have learned.

"Readers, you got some significant reading done today. Some of you watched digital texts, others of you read print ones. I especially want to compliment you on resisting taking extremely detailed notes at this stage. Instead, you got a lot of reading done, and captured some big ideas in your notes.

"Before you talk to a partner, you want to consider what most struck you today as you were reading. Look over your notes, and think about what you want to share and talk about. That way, when you talk with your study partner, you can synthesize your best thinking together.

"So, think for a moment. What seems most important from what you learned today? When you have an idea, explain to your partner. Try to explain not only what you learned, but why it's *important*."

Inspire kids to set their own homework for tonight—to finish a text, or to preview or start a new one.

After kids talked for a few minutes, I said, "Nice work, partners. Before you finish, can you take a moment and set your own homework tonight? Try to do at least fifteen minutes more research—continue to get the big picture of your topic. Are you going to finish a text you started today? Read a new one? Look at your text set and tell your partner what you'll do tonight. You'll start tomorrow by teaching someone about what you learn tonight."

SESSION 1 HOMEWORK

JOTTING INITIAL BIG IDEAS

Set your own homework tonight, to read or watch a text for about fifteen minutes, then jot one or two big ideas, so that you are ready to teach a partner. Be ready to share your work at the start of class tomorrow.

Becoming a Proficient Study Partner

MINILESSON

CONNECTION

Give students a moment to share the continuing research homework they gave themselves last night. Compliment them on the significance of doing more outside of school.

"Researchers, last night, you set your own homework, to do about fifteen more minutes of research. Take a moment now to review whatever you thought about and jotted, then explain what you learned to your partner."

I visited one or two partnerships as they did this work, then reconvened students.

"While you were sharing your research into your topic, I was researching you. First, I want to compliment you all. A lot of you are already on your second text. And you did some extra work last night, either finishing a text, or starting a new one. Learning to do a bit more outside of class, on your own, is a game changer for how you'll do in school. When you're in high school and college, don't wait for

23

a teacher to assign you work. Do a bit on your own, then talk about it with other students and your teacher. You'll see, it's not just that you'll know more, it's that people will also treat you differently, because it shows you care."

Give students a tip: it's different when you are studying with a partner or group than when you are working alone.

"I also want to give you one tip—when you are studying with a partner or group, it's different than when you are working alone. I was interested to see if you would add your partner's learning to your own—did anyone jot down a new idea, or make note of an interesting source that you might read next, after you talked with your research partner? Because you should. Whenever you are working in a study group, now or in college, your learning should be intensified and magnified because you are studying with others."

"You'll be combining and synthesizing your notes at the end of this bend as you get ready to explain an overview of your topic to others. So you want to think now about how you'll gather the most information, because there are several of you studying the same thing."

❖ **Name the teaching point.**

"Today I want to teach you that to get the most out of a study group, it's worth it to think about *how* you'll get more done and support each other. For instance, proficient study partners often talk a lot about what they've learned, actively contribute resources and ideas, and share their notes and study tools."

TEACHING

Share an anecdote about a colleague contributing to your study topic as an example of how study partners find and share resources with a study group.

"Let me give you an example. You know I'm studying free speech, and so in a way, we're all learning a bit about free speech. Free speech is related to all of your topics, because having a voice matters to every activist and researcher.

"Well yesterday, when I was having lunch with other teachers, I was talking about our study. Then today, our eighth-grade science teacher told me she had been thinking about this work, and she had found this article she thought we should add to the free speech text set. It's about what happens when scientists disagree with each other, and how, historically, scientists have sometimes shut each other down and blocked each other's research. It's pretty fascinating."

I showed the article, "The Scientific Importance of Free Speech."

"I had been mostly thinking about free speech as having to do with politics, but this article makes me realize that it's a huge issue in science as well.

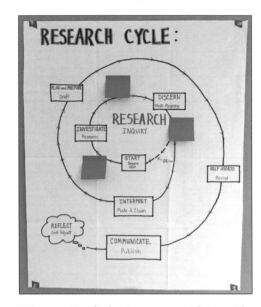

FIG. 2–1 Marc's charts engage students with ways of working and thinking across units and disciplines.

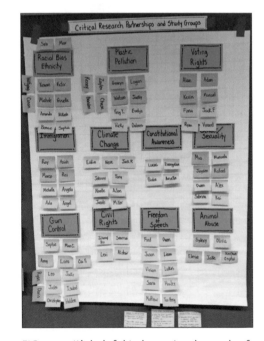

FIG. 2–2 It's helpful to keep visual records of partnerships and study groups.

"That's the kind of thing a great study partner does—finds more resources, and makes them available to the group—especially at this stage, when you're reading to build background knowledge, which means reading as much as possible."

ACTIVE ENGAGEMENT

Invite clubs to share things members have already done that contributed to the study group, and to think of other ideas for how to support their collective learning.

"Will you get together now, not just with your partner, but with your entire study group, and think about other ways that study partners might work so that you learn more together, get more done, and support each other?"

I picked up my notebook. "I'll try to gather some of your thinking as you talk, so we come up with a list of ideas."

Soon kids were talking about finding articles and videos, about sharing new vocabulary, about sharing notebook pages and notes. I jotted. After a bit, I gathered students and shared a list.

"Let me share this "Ways to Actively Contribute to a Study Group" chart with you. Here are some of your ideas." I read it, attributing some ideas to certain students.

"Readers, these are smart ideas. If you do any of these things, your study group will appreciate your efforts. And you'll end up with more notes, more knowledge, more thinking. I'm going to give you one more tip: you can also support study partners emotionally. You can check in on how they're doing, be aware of their schedule, when they can do lots of homework and when they can't, be willing to be supportive, and also be willing to challenge." I added those bullets to our chart.

LINK

Invite kids to reflect and set goals as study partners, and then send them off to work.

"Readers, this work matters, because if one of the skills that lets you be more successful in hard academic classes is building background knowledge, another is getting and being a proficient study partner. In fact, finding study partners can help you build more background knowledge, more quickly. You don't have to already know how to be a great study partner. You can learn to be a great study partner. So, right now, will you look at this list, think a moment, and tell your partner one thing on here that you want to do more of?"

I waited as kids talked.

"Okay, off you go. Before you do, though, take one second to plan your work with your partner. You'll want to use this time to get as much reading done as possible. You should be on your second text today, and moving to a third by the end of the period. Remember, you are choosing accessible texts and reading them rapidly at this stage."

When you gather student thinking and make it more beautiful and organized, it elevates their work. It also lets you continue the work of role-playing kids into academic identities, as you attribute some ideas to one student or another, complimenting them and propping up their academic self-esteem.

You can always add some ideas you wish your students came up with, possibly by saying, "I'm going to add another idea, that will help you be more powerful."

"You'll have time to meet with your club to talk tomorrow. Today, get as much research done as possible. I'll add this new work to our anchor chart as a reminder."

ANCHOR CHART

When immersing oneself in a topic, researchers . . .

- Build background knowledge rapidly by
  - Beginning with accessible and engaging texts
  - Reading thoughtfully, thinking about ideas that are hiding in the text
  - Pausing to note important ideas, information, and questions
- **Work on their role as a study partner by**
  - **Actively contributing**
  - **Supporting partners intellectually and emotionally**
  - **Comparing and challenging new thinking**

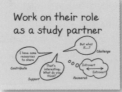

Work on their role as a study partner

FIG. 2–3   Marc gives study groups part of the classroom wall as a place to share research with their study groups—especially those researching a shared topic.

FIG. 2–4   When immersing themselves in a topic, shared notes or a wall space are faster and more collaborative structures than a lot of individual notes.

Increasing Reading Volume While Taking Lean Notes

WHEN KIDS ARE BUILDING BACKGROUND KNOWLEDGE, they need to get a lot of reading done. It can be tricky for them to also contribute in meaningful ways to a study group. Later in the inquiry process it will be okay for them to slow down, to reread, to take deeper notes. But if they do that now, lots of kids will end up reading one or two articles over a few days, and they simply won't know very much background on their topic, or even know what there is to know. It's important that they learn to read across texts fairly rapidly. Here are some tips for helping kids with this process:

Increasing Reading Volume While Taking Lean Notes	
If . . .	**Then you might . . .**
Students need support with choosing texts at their levels . . .	Mark some texts as *background* versus *expert*, or set up club librarians who can help curate collections as *novice*, *proficient*, and *expert*. Then show students how, when reading for background knowledge, it makes sense to read lots of novice texts.
Students need help figuring out ways, other than note-taking, to share information with their club, so they get more reading done . . .	Suggest that kids flag texts as they read, marking important images, charts, or quotes. Then rehearse with them how when they talk with their club, they can open the text to that part and discuss why it seemed important. Often, if you can explain one important visual in a text, it's a way of synthesizing a lot of new thinking.
Students need fast note-taking strategies that don't involve writing long . . .	Offer: • Boxes and bullets • Concept maps (agraphic organizers that capture a main idea and ways that main idea can be divided into subtopics) • Jotting headings or big ideas in the margins on Post-its, and then moving these Post-its into their notebooks
Students need help summarizing and focusing on central ideas . . .	Suggest that just as readers begin to notice emerging themes in fiction, they also notice emerging ideas that rise to the surface across nonfiction texts. You might suggest they jot these ideas on different-colored Post-its, and then simply note when these ideas emerge in different texts, so they have a system for going back to these parts in their texts later.

Comparing and Contrasting New Knowledge

Guide partnerships to notice not only similarities in what they are learning across texts, but also differences as well.

"Readers, why don't you take a moment to compare what you learned today with a partner? Have the texts you read nearby, and any notes you took. Really try to summarize what you learned, and practice those goals you have, for being an active study partner."

After kids talked for a moment, I offered a tip. "Readers, as I listen to you, I want to offer you one tip. You are becoming skilled at comparing what you've learned. You often agree, and you add on to what each other is saying. Will you also try to *contrast* what you've learned, pointing out information or ideas that are different? Remember that you want to push each other's learning, and extend it."

After another minute, I turned students' attention to the chart we had made that day, of ways to contribute to study groups. "Researchers, tomorrow you'll have a chance for a long discussion with your research club, where you can really teach each other what you've learned, and show each other what you've done. Will you look over this list, and set yourself a homework task for tonight?"

Ways to Actively Contribute to a Study Group

Find new resources	Preview texts and label them – create annotated bibliographies
Read something and teach the group	Suggest texts the whole study group should read
Share notes and tools – timelines, flow-charts, diagrams	Compare ideas and thinking with study partners
Check in with study partners, offering support	Question and challenge each other to deepen thinking

SESSION 2 HOMEWORK

PLANNING FOR A GROUP SESSION

Today you assigned yourself a task from the list of ways to contribute to study groups. Tomorrow, you'll be meeting with your whole study group to bring together what you've learned so far. Bring something to share with your club tomorrow—a set of notes, an annotated text, a learning tool, something that will contribute to your study group.

social dynamic of study group

Tapping the Power of Introverts and Extroverts in Collaborative Work

IN THIS SESSION

TODAY you'll teach your students about some of Susan Cain's research on introversion and extroversion. You'll invite students to think about where they place themselves on this continuum (as well as how this placement is often fluid and situational), and you'll provide practical coaching for accessing and increasing the strengths of more introverted and more extroverted students inside of academic collaborations.

TODAY YOUR STUDENTS will consider their own tendencies, especially in collaborative academic situations, toward introversion or extroversion, and how to tap their strengths, reflecting individually and with a partner. They will also review previously read texts and notes as a means to plan for discussion. Study groups will meet today.

GETTING READY

✔ You'll share a continuum of extrovert to introvert, which you can create with some chart paper and large Post-its, or on the document camera or Smart Board (see Teaching).

✔ You'll coach introverts on ways to get into discussions, and extroverts on ways to facilitate discussions, using a series of tips and prompts (see Conferring and Small-Group Work).

✔ Be prepared to add to the "When immersing oneself in a topic, researchers . . . " anchor chart (see Share).

Helping students identify benefits of introverts / extroverts

MINILESSON

CONNECTION

Alert students that they will be meeting with their study group today, and invite them to think about what they'll bring to the group.

"Researchers, let's think for a moment about where you are in your process of building background knowledge. So far, you've worked a bit on your own, in class and outside of school, and you've worked a bit with a partner. Most of you are in your third text now, and some of you, because you looked at infographics or shorter texts, are on your fourth.

"Today you'll have time to really dive into a deep discussion with your study group, where you share and deepen each other's knowledge. As you prepare for that work, it's worth it to think not only about what ideas and information you bring, but also what parts of yourself you bring to this kind of collaborative work."

❖ **Name the teaching point.**

"Today I want to teach you that whenever you are working collaboratively, you inevitably bring part of yourself to the work. In particular, you bring your strengths as being more introverted or extroverted in collaborative academic situations. Reflecting on these ways of being can help you harness your strengths, and work through any challenges."

TEACHING AND ACTIVE ENGAGEMENT

Give an explanation of an extrovert to introvert continuum, showing kids some descriptors as you explain.

"Let me show you what I mean. I have a diagram here, a kind of continuum from extrovert to introvert."

I showed the diagram.

"These aren't fixed categories, but in general, in situations where you're more of an extrovert, chances are these things are true for you: noise doesn't bother you, you like working in groups, you can speak quickly in the groups, you share your thoughts easily." As I spoke I put up Post-its on the diagram.

"In situations where you're more of an introvert, chances are these things are true: you find noise hard, you sometimes crave solitude, you like working alone or in very small groups, you often think more than you say aloud to the group."

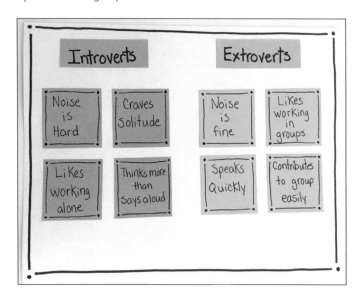

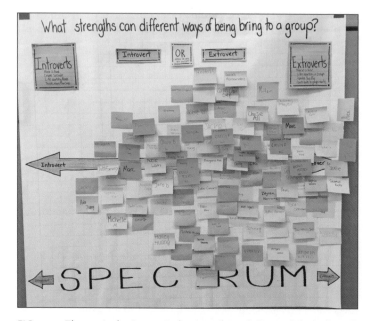

FIG. 3–1   These students created a coauthored chart of their shared and individual ways of being.

Demonstrate how you self-assess your own tendency toward one end or the other of the continuum; reflect on particular strengths you bring and challenges you face in group settings.

"For me, for instance," I took up a Post-it labeled *me* and moved it as I spoke. "In school, I often act like an extrovert, because I feel as if school kind of demands that. But inside, and in social situations, I'm secretly an introvert. I love being alone. I don't like a lot of noise. I often think a lot of things that I don't necessarily say. So for me, I often get a lot done on my own, but then in the group, I have to work harder to engage, and to make sure I don't lean back and kind of create my own quiet space." I could see some kids nodding already.

Invite students to reflect quietly and then to share with a partner, thinking about where they tend to fit on this continuum. Encourage them to think about situation and code-switching as well.

"Take a moment. Where do you see yourself on this continuum, when you're in school, and especially working in groups? What does that mean for you?"

Almost immediately, kids were saying things like, "I'm way over there . . ." or "With my friends I'm more . . . but in class I'm more . . ." or "I think I'm in between" or "I can be both."

I moved among them, saying things like, "Oh, so you code-switch, you go back and forth?" and "Oh, maybe you're an ambivert, you're both," or "Hmm, . . . that does sound like you're an extrovert!"

After a few minutes, I encouraged kids to shift to thinking about what strengths and challenges they faced, saying things like, "What might this mean for you?"

Help students reflect on how bringing more self-knowledge to their group interactions can help them individually, and can help them as a group.

"I can hear how self-reflective you are being. You really know yourselves. Some of you are saying you are definitely introverts, at least in this kind of situation, which makes group interactions more challenging, and you'll need to think about ways to bring your strengths to the group. Some of you are extroverts, and you need to harness your strengths on behalf of the group.

"So now, let's shift to thinking about . . . what are some particular strengths of introverts?"

Soon hands were raised, and I called on kids. As they spoke, I charted.

Then I asked, "What about extroverts?"

Soon we had a small chart.

FIG. 3–2   It's fascinating to see kids reflect on their ways of being.

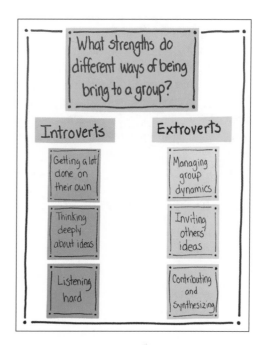

"This is some important thinking, readers. When you do anything, you bring your whole self to that endeavor. And when it's a group activity you're participating in, whether it's a school one or a social one, there are particular challenges, and you want to reflect on and then help each other bring out all your particular strengths."

LINK

Suggest that students spend about ten minutes preparing for their discussion, by both reviewing their content and thinking about the strengths they'll bring to their study group.

"In about ten minutes, you'll meet with your study group. Will you spend this time first, preparing for that discussion? Prepare your content—what you want to say—by looking over your texts, and any jotting that you've done about the big picture, the important concepts related to your topic. *And* prepare for how you'll bring your ways of being to your group.

"You won't be reading more today. Instead, you're reviewing what you've learned so far, and organizing any texts or notes you want to have on hand as you talk with your group. So far, you've mostly focused on boxes and bullets as a way of taking lean notes, but later this week your group will make decisions about flowcharts, lists, diagrams, and other ways of visualizing information to be able to present it, so you should start thinking about that now: what are the big, important ideas and parts and controversies of your topic and how will you best be able to represent them so others can understand them quickly and well?

"Look at the clock. In ten minutes you will find your group and share your content—and think about how you function as a study group. Pay attention to all the background knowledge you've built through research, and pay attention to each other."

ANCHOR CHART

When immersing oneself in a topic, researchers . . .

- Build background knowledge rapidly by
  - Beginning with accessible and engaging texts
  - Reading thoughtfully, thinking about ideas that are hiding in the text
  - Pausing to note important ideas, information, and questions
- Work on their role as a study partner by
  - Actively contributing
  - Supporting partners intellectually and emotionally
  - Comparing and challenging new thinking
  - **Researching and adding to their own ways of being in academic situations**

Social Engineering to Build Social and Academic Capital

IN *OUTLIERS*, Malcolm Gladwell talks about Oppenheimer and Langdon, who both had genius level IQs. Oppenheimer ends up influencing the human race, and Langdon ends up living alone in a cabin. Gladwell attributes this difference to their social intelligence—Oppenheimer was able to function fluently in groups, he was able to persuade others, he found it easy to rebound from controversy. Langdon was an extreme introvert, who found it almost impossible to communicate with others.

School rewards extroverts. Susan Cain, in her TED talk, book, and YA Book, *Quiet Power*, reminds us that extroverts aren't better people, nor do they think more deeply, or contribute more overall to the human condition, than introverts. It's just that in social environments like school, and in collaborative structures such as clubs, extroverts flourish more easily than introverts.

Some kids are situational introverts. They may be language learners; extroverts on the playground and cafeteria, but find themselves language-based introverts in the classroom. They may be cultural-based introverts, who are adapting to a classroom environment that feels alienating or strange, without relevances to a familiar culture. They may be situational introverts for gendered or other identity reasons, kids who in other environments engage actively, but withdraw in this particular intense, collaborative, academic scenario.

In our work in classrooms this past year, we researched student interactions in clubs and small groups, and invited students to research and reflect as well. From this research we were able to come up with some ways of coaching introverts to engage in collaborative academic interactions, and ways of coaching extroverts to facilitate these interactions and manage their own. Usually we pull kids who identified as introverts, and coach them with these tips, which we jot on Post-its for them, and then we do the same for extroverts.

Tips for Introverts (how to get into the discussion)	Tips for Extroverts (how to facilitate the discussion)
It's easier to start a discussion than it is to jump into a discussion that is moving quickly. Offer to begin. • "Could I begin, today? I thought we could start with . . ."	Give positive affirmation when quieter partners contribute. Make them glad they jumped in. • "That's an interesting point . . ." • "I didn't think about that; let's talk about that now . . ."
It's okay to suggest that a club pause to think or students go back to their notes. Suggest a quiet moment. • "Can we take a moment to go back to our notes, and to think about some of the ideas we've talked about?"	Suggest the club pause, and literally look at a quieter partners' notes. Suggest talking about something they've jotted. • "So-and-so has this in her notes. Let's talk about that . . ."

Tips for Introverts (how to get into the discussion)	Tips for Extroverts (how to facilitate the discussion)
It's also okay to go back to an idea that came up earlier, even if the discussion has moved on. Suggest returning to an earlier idea. • "I'd like to go back to something that . . . said . . ."	Notice when someone is trying to get into the conversation, by noticing their body language. Even if the conversation has moved on, invite them in. • "It looked like you were thinking something, did you agree, or were you thinking something different?"
It's fine to push back on being asked to contribute immediately. You can say you'd like a moment. • "I need a moment to think about that. Can you give me a minute . . ."	It is fine for you to talk and to lead the talk, AND use your influence to bring along others, to strengthen the group. Suggest quiet moments at times. • "Maybe we should take a quiet moment, to gather our thoughts."

FIG. 3–3   Kai works quietly, enjoying the chance to get a lot done on her own.

Study Groups Consolidate Their Sources and Their Research

Set students up to meet with their study groups, and give them some coaching on starting with reviewing texts, then moving on to describing what they've learned.

"Researchers, take a moment to look over your notes and review the texts you've read so far. In a moment, you'll meet with your study group. I want to give you a few tips about trying to consolidate learning with a study group.

"Often, it's useful first to review the texts you each read, so you have an idea what sources you've delved into so far. You might tell each other which sources are particularly useful, that others might want to read, for instance.

"Then, you'll want to describe what you've learned. You'll want to use your notes and any annotations to prompt your thinking. Then, as you talk, pay special attention to connections between what you've each read. Those are some methods for how study groups consolidate their learning and get more done together than they would alone."

Before class ended, I interrupted study groups, saying, "Study groups, it's important that you set your own homework. Think about what sources you've read and which you haven't, what areas of your topic you feel like you know a lot about, and what you want to know more about. Then work with your study group to set your own homework, assuming that you'll do about twenty minutes of work tonight."

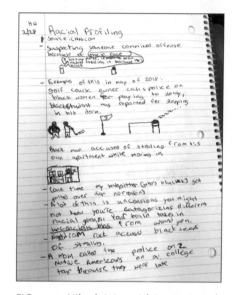

FIG. 3–4   Nikash jots quick impassioned notes as he researches.

SESSION 3 HOMEWORK

 FOLLOWING UP ON RESEARCH PLANS

Today, you met with your study group to review and consolidate what you've learned so far. You also set your own homework, for what you want to research next. Take about twenty minutes to research, including jotting some lean notes to hold onto your thinking.

Conceptual Vocabulary Sorts

GETTING READY

✔ Students need to sit with their research groups. You'll give students slips of paper or cards, markers, and envelopes (see Connection).

✔ Prepare an envelope containing a set of cards with vocabulary terms and phrases related to the class demonstration topic of free speech, and include some blank cards so that you can add additional terms (see Teaching).

✔ Have Post-it notes and markers on hand for creating categories for the sort (see Teaching).

✔ Be prepared to add to the "When immersing oneself in a topic, researchers . . ." anchor chart (see Link).

✔ For conferring and small-group work, you may choose to provide some students with starter sets of words (see Conferring and Small-Group Work).

IN THIS SESSION

TODAY you'll teach students that as they learn about a new topic it will be helpful to develop a system to both gather and begin to work with new vocabulary. One way to do this is to gather important topic-related terms and then try a variety of conceptual sorts to study this new vocabulary.

vocab systems?

TODAY YOUR STUDENTS will have an opportunity to study new vocabulary by sorting words and terms conceptually. They will first practice by using terms related to the class demonstration study of free speech, and then will work in their study groups to gather and sort vocabulary related to their group topics. After they finish this vocabulary work, students will work on setting up their own systems in their notebooks and/or return to their text sets and continue reading. Study groups will meet today.

MINILESSON

CONNECTION

Invite students to reflect on and then jot any domain-specific words, terms, or phrases they have encountered as they have begun to study their topic.

"Researchers, for the last few days you have been gathering with your study groups, discussing what you have learned, and growing your thinking together. As you did so, I noticed you using a lot of vocabulary that was either new words, or they were words you were using in new ways. That's an important skill—the skill of learning the expert vocabulary of what you're studying. It will help you join conversations at a more expert level, and be more authoritative in your speaking and writing. A lot of us were struck by the expert vocabulary, for instance, that Xiuhtezcatl used when he talked about fracking—it's probably a reason that adults took him so seriously."

I handed envelopes with slips of paper inside, and markers, to students.

"I want to try something with you right now. Each of your study groups has an envelope with slips of blank paper and some markers. Will you each take some slips of paper, and will you jot down any words or terms that seem important to the topic you are studying? It doesn't have to be words that are especially hard or new, it's any words or phrases or terms that are important, that would be interesting to talk about.

"I'll do it too."

As students worked. I jotted on slips of paper (or cards, or Post-its) that I could display.

Public schools

Tinker v Des Moines

Supreme Court cases

Civil liberties

Civil disobedience

Constitution

"Take a second now and compare with your club. Show each other your words, then put your words together in the envelope for your club."

After a moment I added, "You're probably wondering why we're doing this—why are we jotting words on slips of paper, instead of starting some kind of glossary or list in our notebooks?"

🍀 **Name the teaching point.**

"Researchers, whenever you are studying something new, it can be extraordinarily helpful to develop a system for gathering significant vocabulary. Often, it's helpful to collect significant terms in ways that will let you practice conceptual sorting, where you sort words under a variety of categories."

Teachers, we've also done these conceptual sorts using small Post-its instead of slips of paper. Students lay these Post-its on the desk or on white paper, and then they can assemble them in their notebooks as well. This method works very well in class. Later, these Post-its sometimes lose their stickiness, which is why we also like the long-term method of slips of paper or small cards.

TEACHING

Lead students in a shared inquiry, collecting, sorting, and re-sorting vocabulary related to free speech. Begin by introducing terms related to free speech, and then give students a chance to study them with a partner and add terms as needed.

"Let's try this together for a moment, to get a feel for conceptual sorting. We'll work with words related to free speech."

I displayed my words. "Look these over for a second with your club. What words here are familiar? What other words might you add? Think about the video we watched the other day, as well as any other terms that have come up in social studies or in current events. Remember, these don't have to be especially complex words or terms, they just need to be important to this topic."

Free expression	ACLU	Supreme Court cases
Violation	Ruling	Reversed decision
Dissenting opinion	Control	Instigate
Public space	Volatile	Viewpoint

"I love how some of you are thinking of vocabulary that has come up in social studies, or in the press. I tried to jot a bunch of the words you added. So now we also have":

Civil liberties	Constitution	Tinker v Des Moines
Political expression	Terrorism	Free speech
Constitutional rights	Litigation	Public school/university
School	Student	Administration

Do a quick demonstration of ways to sort, shifting words around as you demonstrate, giving kids an idea of how they might try this work.

"Watch me do this work for a moment, so you get a feeling for what it looks like to do a conceptual sort. I might, for instance, sort terms based on ones that I know and ones that I don't know." As I spoke, I placed two Post-it notes, one that said *Familiar* and the other *Unfamiliar*, on the document camera and moved some words around under these categories. "Or I might sort by terms that have *Positive* or *Negative* connotations, or by categories, such as *School* and *Court*, or I might sort chronologically." As I spoke, I moved words around, saying them out loud.

I also put some words that I was unsure of in the middle.

"Hmm, . . . I think when I'm unsure of a word, I'll put it in the middle, as worthy of further study."

"Sort It Out" activity

As students talk to each other, gather up some of their words—and you can help them find some as well. If a student says, "There was that court case . . ." you can say, "Oh, you mean Tinker v Des Moines!" If your students have been in social studies units that tackled civil rights, they may have lots of terms. If they haven't, they may only have a few. If you're worried they won't have any, you can give them more words and say, "Which of these should we also include?"

When Freddy Hiebert was with us at Teachers College, she emphasized the difference between memorizing terms and coming to more conceptual understandings. When we try to front-load vocabulary, there's an emphasis on memorizing terms, as kids have little context for those terms. If we help students gather terms as they read and research, and then help them practice conceptual sorts, they come to deeper understandings through seeking, sorting, and explanation.

ACTIVE ENGAGEMENT

Invite study groups to begin sorting their vocabulary, reminding them to add new words as they work.

"Now it's your turn. This is going to be even more interesting with your study. You have the words you each already jotted. The Post-its are for your category labels. And remember, you can use the extra blank slips of paper to write any other related vocabulary words or terms you think of. Try this out for just a couple of minutes—what's one sort you can imagine would be interesting? Would it be different categories? Would it be chronological? Something else?"

As groups worked, I leaned in, encouraging them to add familiar but important words, and to label their sorts. When students were unsure precisely what a term meant, I said "Hmm, . . . you should find out more about that, maybe you should put that in the middle . . ."

Invite study groups to share. Then summarize the work, reminding them that they are not just collecting hard, unfamiliar words, but vocabulary terms that are significant to a new study, and sometimes, new thinking.

"Okay study groups, take a moment to compare with groups on either side of you. Did they sort exactly the same as you, or differently? Did you come to any new thinking?"

LINK

Set kids up to work in their study groups to continue to collect vocabulary terms and try conceptual sorts inside their own chosen topics. Remind students that they can return to texts to find more terms.

"Researchers, let's clarify what your work will look like today. First, you'll go off with your study group, and think about other words and phrases you want to add. You might return to your notes or texts. Then, you'll try some different conceptual sorts, working together to think about different ways to sort these words. As you sort, you'll have lots of conversation about why words should go in one category or another, and other words you might include. You'll probably want to try two or three different ways to sort the words. Each time you sort, talk with your study group about the words. That will help you learn them well, and will help your study group figure out what you want to find out more about.

"I'm also giving each *member* of the group an envelope with blank slips, so that before you leave today, you can jot the most important words that you personally want to keep in an envelope in your own notebook, so you have a system for keeping track of words you are finding significant.

"When your group feels like you've done enough interesting vocabulary work, then move back into your research—and as you research, be alert to new words and terms you want to collect."

I added to our anchor chart before preparing to support students in this work.

When our colleague Audra Robb was trying this work out with students, she was struck by how often their discussion led to new ideas. The act of sorting led kids to think about new categories, or to think about new relationships, and that seemed to lead them to new thinking as well.

It's helpful if kids develop systems where they can get their words cut and sort them for partner conversations, notebook work, or debates.

When immersing oneself in a topic,
researchers . . .

- Build background knowledge rapidly by
  - Beginning with accessible and engaging texts
  - Reading thoughtfully, thinking about ideas that are hiding
    in the text
  - Pausing to note important ideas, information, and
    questions
- Work on their role as a study partner by
  - Actively contributing
  - Supporting partners intellectually and emotionally
  - Comparing and challenging new thinking
  - Researching and adding to their own ways of being in
    academic situations
- **Work to acquire new vocabulary and concepts by**
  - **Gathering words from the texts they study**
  - **Creating systems so they can sort these terms
    conceptually**
  - **Discussing and explaining terms with study partners**

Work to acquire
new vocabulary and
concepts by...

Gather   Sort   Discuss

Supporting Students in Vocabulary Acquisition

WE'VE TRIED THESE CONCEPTUAL SORTS with classes in social studies, science, and English language arts, and each time, the level of engagement is high. Kids really surprise us with their innovative ways of sorting, with their explanations of terms, and with how they help each other learn and set themselves up to find out more.

Your urge may be to give kids a lot of scaffolds (tell them one way to sort, provide definitions, and so on). We encourage you, instead, to think about a variety of ways to support students that will also work toward engagement and independence.

Supporting students in vocabulary acquisition
Play the role of proficient partner.
When you play the role of a proficient partner, you bring energy, enthusiasm, and knowledge to each club and partnerships, but you don't take over, or even stay very long with any one group. Essentially, you start with one pair or group and you join in, saying something like, "Oh, I'm fascinated by . . . can I join for a bit?" Then as kids begin to suggest words and try sorts, your comments are deliberately complimentary and interested. "Oh, that's so interesting, let's definitely try that." You encourage kids to explain and talk about terms. You also model what you do when you're unsure of a term; you might say, "Hmm, . . . I think I need to find out more about that one, let's put it over here, and find out more later." You might add some vocabulary words rapidly, saying, "Should we include . . . and . . . and . . . ?!"
Then you move to the next group, and join in. You'll have a sense of whether a group needs your energy to move the sort along, or simply to keep them excited. Often, you'll find they don't really need you, and you can research what kids are doing well.
Provide lean scaffolds to help some kids get started.
For students who may need more support, there are a few concrete ways to help them get started. One is to provide words as a starter set of terms. Include plenty of vocabulary that is important in their study, but the words aren't hard. Words like *press*, *journalism*, *point of view*, for instance, or for a group studying voting rights, words like *vote*, *voter*, *political party*, *voting booth*, *election* are worth talking about as concepts in a historical study.
You can also support kids by having some Post-its jotted with possible categories to sort by, including:
Themes
Chronology
Positive connotations /Negative connotations
Abstract/Concrete

Another scaffold, especially for sorts in science and history, is to provide words in more than one language—you might have English on one side, and Spanish on the other, for instance. When kids are learning content, we want their level of knowledge to build as rapidly as possible, and accessing their first language can help them deepen their conceptual understanding.

We also want to build academic vocabulary in multiple literacies, so that kids become as powerful as possible as they continue to grow inside of multiple literacies.

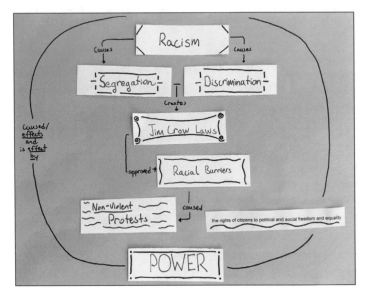

FIG. 4–1   This study group turned their conceptual vocabulary sort into idea development, forging connections between terms.

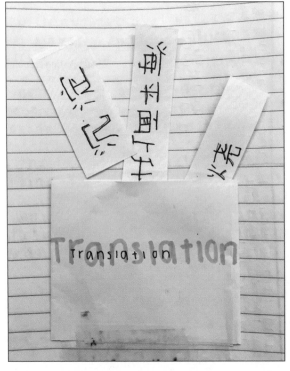

FIG. 4–2   Ailan creates a system to collect vocabulary in more than one language.

Deepening Understanding of Secondary and Contextual Meanings of Words

Give study groups an opportunity to share their terms with other groups.

"Researchers, you did some really interesting sorts today. I've been circulating while you're working, and it's especially interesting to see how groups that are studying similar topics chose different ways to sort, or came up with different vocabulary words. So let's take a moment to compare your sorting with that of another group. If you like their ideas, jot them down somewhere for the next time you sort. Turn to a club near you, and explain some of your sorts, and some of your terms—why are these words important?"

After groups spent a few minutes doing this, I interrupted.

Draw students' attention to the intricacies of domain-specific vocabulary, and how the same term can mean different things in different disciplines or contexts.

"Readers, can I have your eyes on me? I want to draw your attention to some important vocabulary work you are doing.

"Some of you are noticing that some of the words and phrases you're studying have more than one meaning. Sometimes, it's that the words themselves mean different things in different disciplines. Like, the word *cell* can mean a prison cell, or it can also mean a resistance group if you're studying civil rights, or it could mean a plant cell if you're studying photosynthesis.

"And other times, a word comes to mean different things depending on the historical perspective. Like the word *rebel*, or *traitor*, or *patriot* meant something different to people on different sides of the American Revolution.

"Will you turn back to your study group? Talk about any words that have contextual meanings, or ones where the meaning signifies something different to different people, in different times."

Soon kids were talking about words like *right*, *native*, *border*, and so on.

Set kids up to create their own collections of words.

When there were about five minutes left in class, I interrupted. "Researchers, you have a fabulous collection of words. Make sure one of you keeps this collection, and you can add to it when you are working together as a study group, so that as your knowledge deepens, you are better able to have expert, sophisticated discussions. In a few days, you'll be sharing what you have learned about your topic, and it will be important that you think about how to include this expert vocabulary when you are teaching others. After all, using expert terminology will make you so much more authoritative in your writing and speaking.

"You will also want your own personal collection—not just for this study, but anytime you are studying something new. So tonight, jot the words that seem most important to have in your own collection. You can create your own envelope, or you can devise your own system, using Post-its, or technology, or whatever you'd like. You can start now."

SESSION 4 HOMEWORK

SOLIDIFYING CONCEPTUAL SORTING SYSTEMS

Readers, today in class, you practiced some conceptual sorts with your study group. As you continue on with your studies, in this class and in high school, you'll want to do this work, especially when you are building background knowledge on a new topic. Tonight, solidify the system you'll use, and make sure it allows for rapid sorting in different ways. Use it to organize your own personal collection of words that are significant to your research study—not necessarily hard or unfamiliar terms, but ones that matter to this topic. Come tomorrow with words and phrases to talk about with your group.

Advanced Notebook Work
Synthesis Pages

TODAY you'll teach students that successful researchers don't just collect information about their topic, they also go back and rethink. You'll lead them in an inquiry of mentor notebook pages to inspire students to develop the habit of going back into their notes to synthesize their learning. It's possible that you may want to give two periods to this work. Plan accordingly!

TODAY YOUR STUDENTS will study a variety of mentor notebook pages, and then will have time to look over the on-the-run lean notes they've taken so far and reorganize their learning into new synthesis pages. Students will share their work in a gallery walk. Study groups will not meet today.

✔ Invite students to sit with partners in the meeting area, with homework and notebooks (see Connection).

✔ Prepare a chart "High-Leverage Academic Habits" (see Connection).

✔ Be prepared to share visuals of notebook pages of some famous thinkers. You may also decide to provision kids with this resource on Google Classroom or another platform (see Teaching).

✔ Prepare to start a chart, "How Do Great Thinkers Use Their Notebooks?" (see Teaching and Share).

✔ Prepare to share visuals of other students' science and social studies notebook pages (see Active Engagement).

✔ Provision students with colored pencils, tape, Post-its, glue sticks, scissors (see Link).

✔ Be prepared to add on to the "When immersing oneself in a topic, researchers . . ." anchor chart (see Share).

MINILESSON

CONNECTION

Invite partners to share the work they've done so far in this bend, and as they do so, study the ways they've taken notes or used their notebooks so far.

"Researchers, will you open your notebook, and show your partner the work you've done so far, as you've immersed yourself in your topic? Share your vocabulary work, your summarizing, and any other notes you've taken."

I looked over kids' shoulders as they shared.

"Let's come back together. It's interesting to see the ways you've taken notes and annotated. Some of you did some annotating directly on an article. Some of you have notebook pages where you jotted short summaries. Others of you took notes in other ways. I see some concept maps and some T-charts."

Give kids feedback, and let them know the significance of learning to keep a notebook—any kind of notebook—as a place to both gather information and think about ideas.

"When we started this study, I shared some research with you, about how kids who do very well in hard academic classes in high school and college often develop a few very important habits. I told you that one of those habits was that these kids do more outside of school—they read up on topics, they add to their background knowledge on their own. Well, there are two more habits that appear again and again when researchers interview kids who do very well academically." I showed a quick chart, "High-Leverage Academic Habits."

"Turn and tell your partner—which of these habits have you already developed, and what could you get better at?"

I waited while partners talked, then said, "I hear a lot of you saying you feel like you're getting pretty good at building background knowledge. And you're all becoming better study partners. So let's tackle the notebook and note-taking. Some of you take copious, perhaps too copious, notes. Others of you barely jot. So the question we want to ask is: What kind of notes are worth it? What do great research notebooks look like?"

❖ Name the teaching point.

"Today I want to teach you that the most successful students don't just collect information in their notes. They also reread and reorganize their notes to synthesize their learning. One way to do this is to pause now and then, look back over and perhaps annotate your notes, and create new synthesis pages."

TEACHING

Launch an inquiry into ways great thinkers use their notebooks. Begin by inviting students to study the notebook pages of some famous thinkers, and pose an inquiry question.

"I have a few notebook pages from some famous thinkers. Let's take a look at them!"

I displayed these.

"As you look at these notebook pages, will you consider this inquiry question?"

How do these thinkers use their notebooks in interesting ways?

"Talk to your partner. What are these thinkers doing here? What do you notice about their notebook pages?"

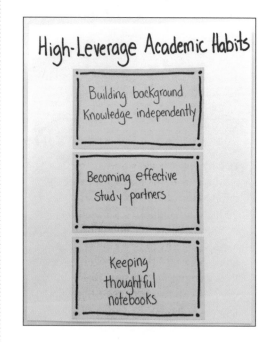

Give students a moment to talk, and then summarize some of the ways these thinkers use notes and notebooks. Point out interesting parts of the mentors as you do so.

"I heard you say that it looks like sometimes thinkers use notebooks to hold onto new information. For example, it looks like Jane Goodall wanted to sketch her observations of the animals she was learning about. And on Lewis and Clark's journey, Clark wanted to record some of the flora and fauna, so he made a careful sketch, with notes around it that show how wondrous he found these creatures. It looks like Dr. Martin Luther King is drafting some of his ideas. It looks like Thomas Edison is figuring out some new thinking—he's planning, and innovating ideas. As is Da Vinci. And it appears he's seeing connections, too, between all these projectile weapons. Some of you knew Darwin's famous cladogram, where he visualizes how species change."

I started a quick chart.

Doing a little "curating" is really helpful when you share mentor notebook pages. Talking lightly about what you're struck by helps kids see more and consider moves they might make. Carry this curating over to studying new student notebook pages as well.

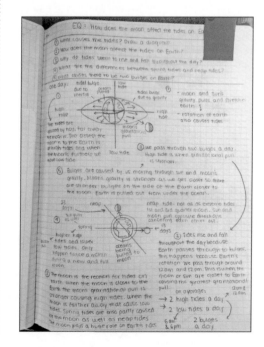

ACTIVE ENGAGEMENT

Introduce some student notebook pages, and invite kids to continue their inquiry, asking the same question about how these thinkers use their notebooks.

"Now let's look at some great student synthesis pages. Take a look at these, and ask yourself that same question: How do these thinkers use their notebooks in interesting ways?"

I displayed student notebook pages.

"Go ahead, talk to your partner. What are these students doing in these notebook pages? What are you impressed by here?"

I gave students time to talk to each other as they studied these pages.

Emphasize the synthesis work in these notebook pages, as well as their recursive quality—the way students went back in to rethink, reorganize, visualize. Point out that these pages do not represent on-the-run fast jotting, but are synthesis pages.

"Researchers, these notebook pages aren't the kinds of notes you take when you are reading a text for the first time. They're not fast, on-the-run jottings. These notebook pages reflect a thinker who has moved on from fast jots, and now is reflecting and synthesizing. And a lot of you are struck by how these students also *care* about what they've learned. You can see it in the ways they've redone their notes with images, and annotations, and diagrams."

I pointed to images as I curated. "You can see how this student added in an image; maybe she thought that would make this research more memorable. This other student went back into her notes and transformed them by adding new thinking in different colors. This student reorganized his notes as a timeline—and then added graphic imagery around it. This student created text features to highlight the cycles of the moon, to layer information.

"Here's the thing. While the notes you take as you read are lean and fast, eventually you know enough that it's helpful to do what these thinkers did, which is to pause, rethink, and synthesize what you've learned so far. That's when going back and creating a new synthesis page or two can be really helpful."

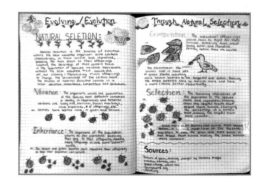

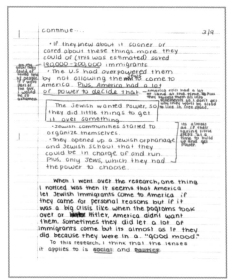

Give kids some tips about how students typically go about working on these kinds of pages.

"To do this kind of notebook work, in any class, you go back into your notes. You review any notes you made, which might be T-charts, or boxes and bullets, or brief jottings. Then, you create a new page or two where you synthesize what you've learned so far."

LINK

Give students a bit of time to plan their work, helping them make decisions about extensive annotating or new synthesis pages. Let students know they'll have a gallery walk at the end of the period.

"I'm going to give you a moment to plan your work for today. At the end of the period we'll have a gallery walk, and each of you will share one or two notebook pages, both to celebrate your work and so we can learn from each other. For a lot of you, this will be the first time you're doing this kind of advanced notebook work, work that is something college students learn to do. So don't worry about it being perfect. There is no perfect. Instead, think about what information and ideas you're finding most fascinating, and imagine how you want use your notebook to pull together that learning and share that thinking with others. We're getting close to the end of this bend of the unit, so your notebook synthesis pages will help you begin to think about what parts or ideas about your topic are the most important to share with others.

"Take a moment now to plan with your partner. Think about: What ideas and information do you want to synthesize? How might you go about that? Which of these notebook entries might serve as a bit of a mentor text?

"As soon as you're ready, off you go. There are colored pencils, tape, Post-its, glue sticks, scissors here. You also have access to the notes you've taken so far and to the texts you've read. If you need to talk to your partner or to me, stay here for a moment, until you have a clear plan."

Teachers, you can decide if you want to give two periods to this work. If it's new to your students, then it might be worth it to give them time to really practice synthesizing, as it's a very high-leverage study skill that strong students do on their own and other students don't think to do. If your kids have already been keeping great science and social studies notebooks, then a single period will be enough for them to capture something important about what they've learned so far.

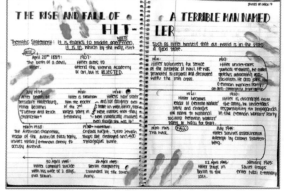

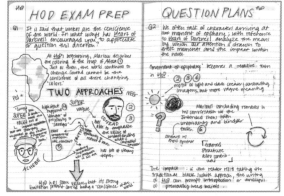

Supporting a Range of Thinkers and Writers in Advanced Notebook Work

SOME OF YOUR KIDS will fly with this work. They'll be eager to add text features, to create graphics, to turn their notebook into an art project. Those kids will need you to help them keep an eye on the big goal, which is to synthesize knowledge. Other students will be apprehensive that they aren't "artistic," or "neat." They'll need you to clarify that neatness and higher-order thinking are not correlated, and that Einstein's notes, and Darwin's notes, often seem scrawled—but the thinking inside these notes is significant. Here are some ways you can coach kids:

Supporting a Range of Thinkers and Writers in Advanced Notebook Work	
If . . .	**Then . . .**
Students need some ideas of how to get started . . .	Suggest they spend some time studying some mentor pages of student notebooks. Have them note parts of these pages that they admire, and choose one as a mentor text. It is fine for students to copy the format of a mentor page, substituting their content. You might sit with students and help them get started, once they choose a mentor text.
Students seem overwhelmed by the scope of the work (both the content and the quality of the mentor notebook pages) . . .	We've provided some simpler synthesis notebook pages in the online resources. This collection is labeled "More Accessible Synthesis Pages." These pages may be more accessible models for some of your students. Have students look through them and find a model they like, and they can use that format for their own work. Also help these students focus on one or two big ideas or essential information.
Students already love the notes they've taken, and think, they're "done" . . .	Remind them that great students and great thinkers don't sit back. They are always rethinking, and one way to force their brain to do that is to go back into their notes, adding in their new thinking, reorganizing and reconceptualizing. It might be helpful to pull together some strong students and have them help challenge each other by working as thought partners.
Students prefer to work with technology rather than paper notebooks . . .	This could be fine! If students have iPads especially, or any form of tablet, then they can create advanced notebook pages that include diagrams, flowcharts, and so on. Some students are also so adept at tech that it's faster and more engaging for them to work this way. Other students may also either take a quick picture of a sketch and insert it into Notability or Evernote or another digital system or use the new digital notebooks that upload easily.

Being Inspired by Peer Mentors
Gallery Walks and Goal-Setting

Set kids up for a gallery walk in which they will study other students' notebook pages. Give some light coaching on ways to respond to peer work and to goal-set.

"Researchers, in just a few minutes we'll begin our gallery walk. Will you use this time to clear your tables and desks of other materials, and lay your notebook open to the page or pages you want to share?"

I waited as students did this.

"Now, as we circulate, bring some Post-its with you. When you see something you admire, jot it down so that you can put it in your notebook afterward, so that you can add it to your own repertoire. You can also leave a note for another student about something you admire.

"Ready? Okay, let's circulate. Find some things you admire. Be on the lookout for the things we noticed in our mentor notebook pages!" I drew students attention back to the "How Do Great Thinkers Use Their Notebooks?" chart we had created earlier.

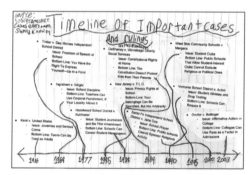

FIG. 5–1   *continued*

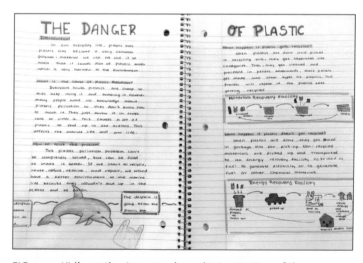

FIG. 5–1   Kid's synthesis pages show the inspiration of the mentors they studied.

After students spent some time circulating, I had them return to their own spots.

"Take a moment. Tell your partner, what were a couple things you liked in some of these synthesis pages? What might you try next time, that you learned from someone here?"

Compliment kids on learning to do more advanced notebook work, and introduce the idea of adding any annotations or features to their notes for homework.

"Researchers, I want to compliment you on the work you did today. Learning to do more advanced notebook work is really learning to do more advanced thinking work. Anytime you are studying something important, it will be worth it to pause every now and then, and create some sort of synthesis page or study guide. Another way to do this kind of thinking that is more 'on the run,' is to add annotations to your notes—to go back in and note connections, or new thinking. That's what you'll try tonight."

I added to our anchor chart.

FIG. 5–2 Jaclyn helps students with protocols for studying mentor notebook pages in science, as well as social studies and ELA.

 ## ANNOTATING YOUR NOTES

Today in class you did more advanced notebook work, creating a new synthesis page. Tonight, practice some lean annotations. Go back to through your notes from the beginning of your topic immersion. Add annotations and additions—you might include your newest thinking, or make connections between parts of your notes, or raise questions, or add more vocabulary. Tomorrow, you'll meet with your study group, and you'll need your best notebook work to share.

A Workday for Research and Note-Taking with Agency

Dear Teachers,

We suggest that what your students could use the most right now is a workday. They have a lot of new skills to practice: reading swiftly and taking lean notes; gathering and sorting vocabulary (and keeping up a system for that); actively contributing to their study group; and going back into their notes to annotate and synthesize.

All of these skills are ones that we want kids to put into play on the day we teach that minilesson; we also want students to internalize these skills so they put them into play across all their academic classes. That means kids need opportunities to practice. It's also tremendously useful to study what kids do when you either don't teach a minilesson, or, as today, you give a micro-lesson. You'll find out what kids are doing with agency, and what they're only doing with prompting and support. And they'll have more time to work.

Here's how your micro-lesson could go. For your *connection*, you might gather kids and have them share what they did for homework. If you're uneasy that enough kids did the homework sufficiently (the homework was to go back into their notebooks and practice annotating their notes), then quietly make note of who did and didn't get that done. Circulate quickly, complimenting, responding to content, and so on.

Then your *teaching point* might sound something like, "Today I want to teach you that whenever you are finding out more about a topic, often what you need most is time to work. When you work, you want to apply all the research skills you've learned, so that your work is as efficient and thoughtful as possible."

In your micro-*teaching*, show students your anchor chart as a reminder. You may, at this point, make small versions of it for them to tuck into their notebooks. Then suggest that just as in a soccer game the coach needs to let the players loose to scrimmage, you too need to let students loose in an academic scrimmage. Let them know that they should:

1. Reflect on what they've learned so far about high-leverage study skills, including working in study groups.
2. Meet with their club to plan their work for the day, including if they will research the whole time, or meet at the end of the period (let them know that clubs will meet in the next session).
3. Get to work, doing their best research work. Aim for researchers to be reading their fourth or fifth text by the end of the day.
4. Be thinking about gathering any more background information they might need on their topic, as the next day they will be drafting an infographic as a means to teach others about their topic.

You may want to visit with study groups as they plan their work, jotting some notes on the efficacy of their plans, who is leading, how they are listening to each other (remember your introvert/extrovert coaching moves), how ambitious they are in terms of volume of reading, and so on. You can pause to give students feedback in the moment, or you can visit several groups rapidly, and then convene them quickly to talk to you.

As kids work, watch how they choose texts, how they take notes. You have a lot of options for *conferring and small-group work* from earlier in the unit that you probably haven't had time to fully put into play. You might look these over—possibly print them and carry them with you. We've made a single online resource for you that is the full collection of small groups and conferences for this bend of the unit—it's in the online resources at the start of Bend 1. We do give you one piece of advice, which is to be lean with your conferring today. Give kids a lot of time to work. Most kids need practice getting a lot of work done. It's one of the most important study and life skills we can help them with.

Study groups can decide on their own method to *share*, and they can set their own homework. Perhaps they want to quickly fill each other in on what they researched. Perhaps they want to choose one text to watch or read for homework. Perhaps they want to create a shared tool. Maybe they want to do another conceptual vocabulary sort. If needed, provide these options, within the frame of "You might choose to . . . or maybe you have another idea . . .what matters is that you learn to set your own agenda, be your own work captains."

It's tremendously interesting to watch kids work independently. Some will surprise you with how steadily they focus, and how they support each other. Some will surprise you with how dependent they are on you for what to do. Try to turn these more dependent kids toward each other, fostering interdependency on their peers, rather than codependency on you. It's lovely to have some time to study your kids as they work.

All the best,
Mary and Marc

FIG. 6–1 As kids research, they can accumulate shared research in one place so that study groups can benefit from each other's work.

Synthesizing Knowledge as Infographics

IN THIS SESSION

TODAY you'll teach students that researchers often transition from finding out more to sharing what they've learned. One way to do that is to synthesize their knowledge and convey it in an infographic.

TODAY YOUR STUDENTS will first study and rank a collection of infographics, and then set out to make their own. They'll become familiar with very easy-to-use software, revisit their notes, and talk with thought partners to make important decisions about what to include and what ideas to highlight in their infographics. If tech is an issue, kids can work by hand. Study groups will meet today.

MINILESSON

CONNECTION

Share with students the idea of digital infographics as a way of pulling together knowledge— and highlighting ideas.

"Researchers, your knowledge about your topic has really grown. You've read a lot of texts. You've watched documentaries and studied a variety of digital texts. You've gathered vocabulary. You've taken lean notes on the run and then synthesized these notes into more meaningful notebook pages. You've learned to go back into your notes and annotate, to constantly add to your thinking. Along the way, you've thought about your role as a study partner inside of a study group, and you've worked to be a better study partner as well as an independent thinker.

GETTING READY

✔ Provision students with two sets of sample infographics—we provide a set on climate change and a set on the Vietnam War, which we suggest you share with kids as printable color PDFs and or PowerPoint/Keynote presentations or Google slides. Links to these infographics are available in the online resources (see Connection and Teaching and Active Engagement).

✔ Invite students to sit with their study groups (see Teaching and Active Engagement).

✔ Make a program or app, or a variety of these, available to students, for creating digital infographics. Free, easy-to-use software includes Piktochart, Canva, and Venngage—and the purchased versions of these programs provide more templates. Or your students can work by hand, in which case you will need to supply paper and markers. We've collected some student samples that are available in the online resources.

✔ Decide, or allow your students to decide, if they will work alone, in partnerships, or in study groups. Note that many of the infographic templates are in built in "parts," so kids can draft parts individually, and then redraft them as one document, since the free versions of these programs don't allow simultaneous document sharing by multiple users. Our students mostly worked in study groups.

✔ It's helpful to have some student digital coaches, who can run quick seminars for other students. Talk to students who are particularly digitally adept, and suggest that they might offer support.

"Today I want to show you a way to use technology to synthesize your thinking and share it with others, in a clear, effective, and engaging way. You can synthesize your knowledge and use a digital tool to create a sophisticated infographic. These infographics can summarize and celebrate your learning so far. They'll also mark a turning point in the inquiry process, one where you've learned quite a bit of background knowledge, and you're ready to begin to share what you know so far."

❖ **Name the teaching point.**

"Today I want to teach you that researchers often move from finding out more to sharing what they've learned. One way to do that is to synthesize your knowledge and convey it in an infographic. To do that work, you'll need to make important decisions about what information to include, what ideas you want to highlight, and what graphics will make your thinking compelling."

TEACHING AND ACTIVE ENGAGEMENT

Begin with an inquiry, inviting students to do some studying and ranking of mentor infographics.

"To get ready for this work, it makes sense for you to get to know the genre. So let's give you a chance, first to study some infographics, thinking about what makes some of these, or parts of these, particularly effective.

"I have two sets of infographics here. Set A is a set of science infographics that consider climate change. Set B is a set of social science infographics that consider the Vietnam War. Choose a set with your study group. Then take a few minutes, and try to rank these infographics, from less interesting or effective, to more interesting and effective. Talk about what makes each of them engaging and informative."

Soon kids were poring over these digital images, talking about parts they particularly liked. I added in, after a minute, "It may be that you like *part* of one of these. That's okay, you can rank parts if you want."

Reconvene students, and share that there are lots of different ways for infographics to be compelling.

"It's so interesting listening to you. Some of you are drawn to the simpler graphics—there is a clarity about them that's compelling. Some of you are drawn to these infographics that layer a lot of information.

"I want to highlight one point. That is, one thing that makes a lot of these compelling is that there is an underlying idea that the infographic is getting across—it's not just a heap of information. Like this one, 'How to Prevent Climate Change in Your Own Little Way,' is clearly suggesting that there are things ordinary people can do to make a difference. And this on one the Vietnam War clearly intends to show the haunting tragedy of how rapidly these young soldiers often died."

FIG. 7–1 Liam gives the class a seminar on Canva software. Tap the knowledge of your tech experts!

Shift from studying mentors to introducing the software that students may use. Show students that they'll need to take a little time to consider the tools of the software, and more time to consider what they want to include.

"Now that you have an idea of what makes these infographics, or parts of them, compelling, it's going to be so interesting to see what you make. There's a lot of software that provides templates for making infographics. This software is super easy to use—you're going to be able to dive into it quickly.

"Watch the kind of thinking I do as I get started, and in a minute, tell your partner what you noticed."

I opened up Piktochart (or another software program) so kids could see my work, quickly showing kids how I set up my account with my school email, skipped the advertising tips, and chose "Infographic."

"Okay, so it looks like one of these is more like a flowchart or series of steps—that's going to be great if I want to show a sequence of events. Let me think about that. Maybe I could show the sequence of important Supreme Court cases that have tested free speech, that could be fabulous. But, hmm . . ." I pointed to the parts of the template as I spoke, "if I include all the Supreme Court cases, there will be too many, so I could focus on ones having to do with students and school. That way, I could bring out a big idea about school being a testing ground for free speech."

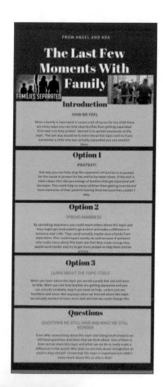

I pointed to another template. "This one starts with a space for an image or information, then you can include a timeline, and then it looks like you can also have a compare-and-contrast part. So if I wanted to use this template I could put the First Amendment in the first box, and then have a timeline of big events and moments that tested free speech. Then at the bottom I could do a comparison of then and now. I have to think more about that. Maybe the idea I could bring out if I created an infographic like this is that the right to free speech is one that is still being tested, it's being tested all the time."

I opened my notebook. "I think I'd like to do just a little drafting here, and then I can move my ideas onto this digital platform. Like, if I focus on the Supreme Court cases where schools were a testing ground for free speech, then maybe . . ." I sketched in my notebook, drafting what the parts of this flowchart might look like.

Ask students to talk about the thinking you did as you got started using the digital tool. Summarize, highlighting the content choices you considered, how you matched those to formatting decisions, the focus on a big idea, and how you used your notebook to draft.

"Take a moment right now and talk to your thinking partner about what you noticed me doing as I considered and planned for my infographic." I gave students a minute to talk and then called the group back together.

"What's important here is not so much what graphics you think are cool. What really matters is what content you want to include, and how certain graphics can help you highlight certain information. Making decisions about what to make big and what to make small, what to include and what to leave out, that's the big work, as is thinking about what big idea you want to bring out.

"Also, before I dove into drafting digitally, I did some quick drafting in my notebook. That's going to let me play with ideas quickly, and also consider what formats or graphics will best help me communicate my focus."

Invite students to do some preliminary thinking and planning with a partner.

"Let's give you a moment to play with this work with a partner. Talk for a moment. What big ideas might you want to bring out in your infographic? And then, what format would help you show this focus? Would you imagine a kind of flowchart, or a timeline, or something with parts? What research do you most want to highlight? Use your notebook to sketch as you talk."

I gave students a few minutes to talk and sketch with a partner, then reconvened the group.

LINK

Review a series of steps students can follow and some guidelines to help them manage their time. Then send students off to work.

"Let's think about what your work will look like today. First, you'll probably want to spend about five minutes getting into the software and looking at some templates. Second, you'll want to look over your notes, and think about what content you most want to focus on. Some of the work you did with your synthesis pages should really help out here. Third, you'll want to use your notebook for some quick drafting. Then, you'll create, using one of these digital tools.

"So let's say, in about five minutes, you should be looking at templates. In about ten minutes, you should be back in your notes, making content decisions, and doing some drafting. In about fifteen to twenty minutes, you'll probably be in the software, drafting digitally.

"If you're intimidated by the software, we have some particularly digitally adept students who can help you get started, or problem solve once you are started. Tomorrow you are going to have an opportunity to share what your group has learned, using your infographic as you talk to help highlight important ideas about your topic. There's a lot to get done, but you are ready! Off you go."

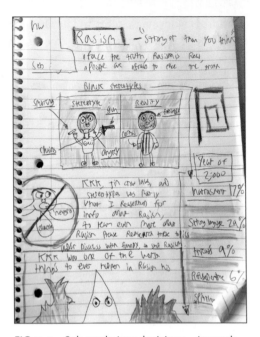

FIG. 7–2 Seb made two decisions—to work alone and to work on paper. Both choices facilitated his deep thinking on this troubling topic. It's important that our classroom structures are flexible, responsive, and personal.

Rising to the Challenge of Collaborative Digital Publishing

THERE ARE A VARIETY OF CHALLENGES that digital drafting poses—and students will be perfectly capable of meeting these challenges, often faster and better than we more "mature" educators. Still, it helps to predict some of the challenges and be prepared for them. Remember to enlist students as coaches, since some of them will have experience with graphic design or just be particularly adept at maneuvering in new software.

Coaching Students to Get Started and Learn on the Run

Some digital learners (of any age) are psychologically intimidated by programs they don't know yet. They want an in-depth tutorial, yet often this in-depth tutorial seems to have little effect on increasing their confidence or independence. There are two approaches that can be helpful. One is a ruthless "just get on and try something, and when you have been in the program and tried navigating a bit, then I will provide some support." This approach follows what Carl Anderson has often talked about, which is that it's often best to confer with writers once they have something on the page—so they don't become codependent, and so you and they can see what they can do.

A second approach is to provide a proficient partner right from the start, one who acts as a tutor/thought partner. This can be a teacher or a peer. The proficient partner gives guiding instructions in a step-by-step way, coaching the user on what to click, what to open, how to move to the next step, so that before they know it, the user is in the program and beginning to use it. They may or may not be fully independent, but at least they are started!

Inspiring Kids to Move beyond Downloading and Pasting

Some pilot teachers suggest that you may even want to forbid students from downloading and pasting in photographs, because kids end up doing that rather randomly, as opposed to thinking carefully about what graphics to include. Anything that is easy (copy and pasting) leads to less consideration than something that takes a moment (previewing art, choosing graphics, and so on).

For students who move quickly into copying and pasting, sit with them and look at some mentor texts again. Suggest they think first about the content they want to convey. Act as a thought partner for ways to convey this content, or engage a partner or group as thought partners. It can also be helpful to clarify that the most significant part of this work is the thinking work it engages the researcher in, not the finished product.

Supporting Kids in Collaboration and Drafting and Redrafting in Parts

Some of the infographic software only allows authors to collaborate in real time if you've purchased the pro version. That means that if they're using the free version and they're collaborating, kids will need to draft quickly in a notebook, and then draft a version of their part digitally, and then be ready to redraft on the shared version on one computer. You may need to support some students in these steps, so they use their time productively.

The good thing about this process is it's real—working collaboratively involves a lot of prewriting and redrafting. Often, the second time kids draft, the process goes more quickly, and they make significant revisions as they draft.

Challenging Students to Convey Ideas, Both Explicit and Implicit

Some of your students will be very ready to bring out some compelling content ideas. For these students, you might suggest that they go back to some of the mentor examples and talk about the implicit as well as explicit ideas these infographics suggest. It can be helpful to remind students that just as a novel or film can have some themes that are obvious, and others that are more hidden, powerful nonfiction can do the same work.

Sometimes it's helpful for kids to talk with a thought partner about some of the ideas that come up pretty quickly inside their topic and to list those, and then to think about ideas that only come up after you've read more.

Preparing to Share and Celebrate: Goal-Setting and Final Steps

Explain the final presentation for the bend and give students an opportunity to make a plan with their study groups as to how they want to share the preparation and presentation.

"Researchers, tomorrow you'll celebrate all the hard work you've done so far. To do this, you'll get together with other study groups and teach about what you've learned, using your infographic and any other notes as a starting point for your talk. Your talk will just be three or four minutes long, and you'll speak about your topic in a way that shares the ideas and information you find most compelling so far.

"That means you'll have the first half of the period to make any finishing touches to your infographics and to rehearse who will talk about what. You'll want to consider what you've learned about the different strengths you bring to study groups, and plan to harness everyone's strengths.

"Take some time now to set some goals for your final steps, so that tomorrow you'll be able to fully share and celebrate. What still needs to be done? How will you divide your talk? What could you each do tonight to be more fully prepared tomorrow?"

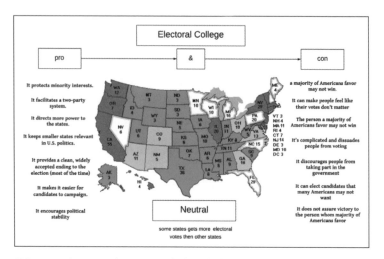

FIG. 7–3 These students grappled with the dilemma of the electoral college.

SESSION 7 HOMEWORK

SYNTHESIZING THINKING TO PREPARE FOR "WATERCOOLER" TALKS

Tomorrow you will have a short amount of time to make any finishing touches to your infographic and to rehearse your talk with your club. Think about what you want to say, and what visuals you want to share. You may lean on your synthesis pages and/or infographics, for instance. Make whatever notes will be helpful. These talks will be like watercooler talks—the kind of informal talks that researchers have with each other in the midst of their research.

Watercooler Talks
Researchers Share Knowledge

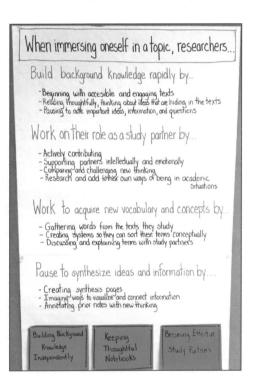

⚇ear Teachers,

There has been a lot of research on the value of watercooler conversations—a metaphor for times when colleagues meet informally and chat about their work and their interests. It turns out that lots of researchers make connections and find support for their work in these quick conversations.

We've fallen in love with watercooler talks as a way for students to share what they have learned, pose questions, teach others, and engage in social connectivity at an intellectual level.

Later in the unit, at the end of the final bend, clubs will publish more polished TED talks, with visual supports and clear arguments, and attention to their language and audience. The talks given today will be shorter and rougher and more conversational. Their talks will be mostly information, although you'll see that some students will already be developing some big ideas from their research.

We suggest that you give students the first half of the period to prepare—to make finishing touches to their infographic and any other visuals they will include and to help study group members prepare. We also suggest you keep these talks to three to four minutes total, which is a lot of talk time for young researchers. We don't suggest that all kids watch as each researcher gives their talk. Instead, either pair up groups or send each study group member out to a different study group.

As kids are preparing, help them think about what they learned about the introvert and extrovert continuum, and help kids find their voices and facilitate their groups with increased awareness and wisdom. Coach them to use their visuals—their infographics, their synthesis pages, and any favorite parts of a text in their talk.

Save the final five to ten minutes for kids to reflect. One way for them to do this is to think, "What have I learned about this thinker, that I want to compliment them on?" It's often lovely to hear kids compliment each other, and they take these compliments to heart, even more than they take our comments. Also, learning to compliment gracefully, specifically, as a way to say, "I see the work you're doing," is a huge step forward in social capital—as is learning to accept these compliments.

You may want to collect notebooks, as we suggested in the assessment section of "An Orientation to the Unit." We've included a student-facing checklist and a teacher rubric in the online resources. We suggest that you may want to assess just the first three items on this tool, in this bend. Then you can assess the following three in the next bend. Probably, you'll want students to self-assess as well, so they can monitor and celebrate their own academic growth. 👆

Compliment yourself, as well. We hope you invited a colleague in to show off the tremendous work that you did in helping your kids grow not only as nonfiction researchers, but overall as academic students. You're increasing equity and access for lots of kids. It's so important.

All the best,
Mary and Marc

Notebook Checklist			
Research Notebooks	Somewhat	Consistently	Yes!
1. I've kept track of sources, developing a system that let's me return to texts and reference them accurately			
2. I've developed a system for collecting significant vocabulary terms and concepts			
3. I've gone back into my notes, annotating, re-organizing, synthesizing			

FIG. 8–1 A sample notebook checklist for Bend I. We provide this and the full checklist and rubric in the online resources. You can, of course, adapt it.

Ethical Research Practices and Internet Literacy

A Letter to Teachers

Dear Colleagues,

Your work will take a turn, now, to engage deeply with the ethics and challenges of researching in a digital age. You'll move students from finding arguments inside their research, to explaining those arguments by researching multiple sides and perspectives, to becoming more critical consumers of media, to taking up informed positions. At the end of the bend, students will flash-debate. The goal of these debates is to move from arguing to win to arguing to learn.

FINDING ARGUMENTS INSIDE RESEARCH TOPICS

You'll start this bend by asking students to consider the disputes inside their topics, and you'll set them to do ethical research, where instead of choosing a side and researching only that side, they continue to research multiple sides, so they can come to an informed position. Some of these arguments will represent different sides, groups, or perspectives. But interestingly, some disputes fall within the same side. Green energy scientists, for instance, all agree that greenhouse gases create a need for new energies—but they have different ideas about whether solar-, hydro-, or wind-powered models will be more effective. Sometimes the disputes or arguments are conditional, as well. It makes more sense, for instance, to support hydro energy in places where fast-flowing water is abundant.

You'll engage students in thinking about internal arguments first through your read-aloud work on free speech, where you and they will come to realize that not everyone agrees on the limits of teen free speech in school. Then students will work with their study groups to tease out the arguments they find interesting inside their own topic. As you do this work, you'll help students consider what makes for a valid argument for continued research; namely, that both sides make rational points, are researchable with available texts, and relevant.

DEEPER NOTE-TAKING

In Bend I, students were reading to build background knowledge. In that kind of immersion, it's important that kids learn to read with a fast and furious attitude, so they get a lot of reading done. They learned to take lean notes, and most of their processing was done through talk rather than note-taking. Now, you'll lead students into deeper notes. We found it to be really helpful and inspiring for students to be able to study mentor notebook pages and notebooks. We've put together a kit in the online resources of secondary-level notebook pages. They are all gorgeous, and you may find that you want to mix these together. We don't really believe in any one single note-taking system, like Cornell notes. We believe that researchers take notes in different ways both for different purposes and because our brains work in different ways. The notes that you'll find in these collections show many different styles. What unites them are two factors—the students are serious about their notes, and they have learned to go back into their notes to rethink, to add on, to synthesize.

COMPREHENDING DIGITAL TEXTS

In her book *Writers Read Better: Nonfiction*, our colleague Colleen Cruz gives some pointed suggestions about supporting digital reading. She suggests teaching kids to: preview the text, make a reading plan, consider hyperlinks and whether to visit these links, and navigating back to the original text after leaving the link. We offer these tips here, in this bend, in small-group work. Keep an eye on your kids' reading—they may need support with their digital reading habits.

CRITICAL INTERNET LITERACIES

The bulk of your teaching in this bend will be critical literacy skills, especially critical Internet literacies. You'll teach students to consider bias in the texts they are reading and in themselves. You'll coach them to read closely for connotative language. You'll teach them then to research the authors and publishing groups of the texts they read. Then you'll alert students to be more aware of confirmation bias in how search engines work and how we *receive* research. Your students will become more alert to fake news, distortion, and confirmation bias.

As media theorist Doug Ruschkoff notes in *Program or Be Programmed*, most teens think of themselves as clients of the Internet and social media. They don't understand that they are consumers, and that their interests and histories are being researched, and that what teens see on the Internet is continually shaped and narrowed by their digital history. Then there is the issue of figuring out if texts are valid and reliable. There has always been fake news, and tabloid news, and propaganda disguised as news, and distorted inflammatory news, from founding father Samuel Adams's prose in the *Boston Gazette* inciting anguish in his fellows to the reporting of the sinking of the *Maine's* playing a pivotal role in U.S. involvement in the Spanish-American War. When we think about how much exposure this generation has to media, it feels really important to raise our students' awareness of the intricate ways in which the Internet raises many ethical issues.

All the best,
Mary and Marc

Read-Aloud

Discerning Arguments and Disputes
inside a Research Topic

IN THIS SESSION

TODAY you'll teach students that ethical researchers notice when people or texts disagree, and they don't just simply choose a side. Instead they gather more information so they can take informed positions.

TODAY YOUR STUDENTS will first practice teasing out internal arguments, including positions, sides, and groups, suggested by an article on teen free speech. Then students will have time to work with their study group to articulate arguments inside their own research topics.

GETTING READY

✔ Display a list of sentence starters students to help students consider arguments inside their topic. Research partners should sit together in the meeting area (see Connection).

✔ Prepare a chart, "Sentence Starters that Lead to Idea-Based Thinking" (see Connection).

✔ Prepare your read-aloud of "High School Tells Student to Remove Antiwar Shirt" (see Conducting the Read-Aloud).

✔ You'll introduce a one-day chart on questions researchers ask to find arguments inside of a research topic titled, "To find arguments inside of topics, researchers ask . . ." (see Conducting the Read-Aloud).

✔ You'll need your own notebook to demonstrate jotting notes during the read-aloud. We share Marc's example in the online resources.

✔ Start a new anchor chart for the bend, "Ethical researchers . . ." (see Link).

✔ Prepare a one-day chart, "When researchers come up with debatable positions, they consider arguments that are . . ." that will guide students as they narrow their topic down to a preliminary argument (see Share).

✔ Have ready large blank Post-its (see Share).

CONNECTION

Review the work kids have done so far by reviewing the big skills they've learned and practiced. Engage kids in talking about their content, using a menu of sentence starters that lead to idea-based thinking.

"It's time for a turn in your research now. So far, you've been immersing yourself in your topic. You've been building background information, becoming more informed. Along the way, you've become more skilled at rapid research and at being an effective study partner. You've also learned to take on-the-run, lean notes; to collect and sort and internalize academic vocabulary; and to review your thinking through synthesis notebook pages. You consolidated much of what you learned into infographics that you shared with others and you gave watercooler talks, teaching others about some of the most important ideas and information in your research topics. You have been busy!

"You know more about the topic you've been studying, and you are more powerful researchers and study partners. Now it's time to dive into new research terrain, the terrain of considering the parts of a research topic that are disputed.

"To get ready for the next bend of this work, try one of these sentence starters, and talk about part of your research for a moment." I displayed the "Sentence Starters that Lead to Idea-Based Thinking" chart and gave students a moment to talk.

After listening for a few minutes, I said, "Listening to you, what's powerful is how you're talking about some of the big ideas that people don't necessarily agree on. This is so important, because insightful researchers are alert to arguments inside their topic."

Shift to naming the new teaching of the bend, and of this session.

"Today I want to teach you that researchers notice when people or texts seem to disagree. Ethical researchers don't simply choose a side or a group, and only research that side. Instead, they try to tease out the various sides and perspectives, and they find out more about all these sides before coming to their own position. Sometimes there are disagreements within a side as well and researchers consider the nuances of different positions.

"This will be the work of this bend. You'll move out of immersion and building background research, and you'll research specific arguments you find interesting inside your topic. At the end of this bend, you'll engage in flash-debates, where you will defend a position. Then you'll move on to more formal TED talks in the next bend. So across this bend you'll want to return to your initial research, figuring out the internal arguments—the sides, the pros and cons, and the voices. You'll have to do closer, more alert reading. And you'll use this research to come to your own activist stance."

CONDUCTING THE READ-ALOUD

Set students up to listen with their notebooks open, ready to jot any internal arguments, sides, or disputes. Read aloud the first part of the article.

"Let's try some of this work together. I've got an article here from the *New York Times* about a teenager who got caught up in a civil liberties case—the courts had to decide if he had the right to say what he wanted to say, and wear what he wanted to wear, in his high school. The headline is: 'High School Tells Student to Remove Antiwar Shirt.'

Sentence Starters that Lead to Idea-based Thinking

 People don't agree about...

 People think differently about this. Some people think... whereas others think...

 A major point of contention in this topic is...

 Conflict comes up most often around...

 Some people think what's most important is... and others think what's most important is...

 A common misconception that some people have is... it turns out that...

"Will you try this work of teasing out what's disputed here? Have your notebooks out so you can do some jotting as we read, whenever you note internal arguments, sides, or disputes. Here are some questions you can ask that will help you find some of these arguments." I pointed to the "To find arguments inside of topics, researchers ask . . ." chart.

"I'll give you one heads-up—this article was written in 2003, when George W. Bush was president, just after 9/11 and just as President Bush was gearing up to send American forces to invade Iraq."

I read:

> Bretton Barber, a high school junior in Dearborn Heights, Mich., who is deeply interested in civil liberties, knew what to do when he was sent home from school on Feb. 17 for wearing a T-shirt with a picture of President Bush and the words "International Terrorist."
>
> First, he called the American Civil Liberties Union. But it being Washington's Birthday, no one answered.
>
> Next, he went on the Internet to reread a Supreme Court case from 1969, *Tinker* v. *Des Moines*, that supported students' freedom of expression. Then he called the Dearborn High School principal to talk about his constitutional rights. And then he called the news media.
>
> "I wore the T-shirt to express my antiwar sentiment," said Mr. Barber, a budding political advocate who joined the A.C.L.U. last year and has been to three antiwar demonstrations in the last month. "In the morning, I got a lot of compliments and no negative feedback. But at lunch, the vice principal came and said I had to turn it inside out or go home. When I asked why, he said I couldn't wear a shirt that promotes terrorism."

I displayed this part of the text. "Take another moment to continue to jot. Look at your questions. What seems disputed here? What groups might be important?" As students did so, I moved the text off and displayed my notebook.

Teachers, when you are reading aloud a challenging text, you'll feel the urge to give kids the text, or display it as you read. Know that dealing with the print actually makes it harder for kids. If the text is above their reading level, listening to it helps their comprehension. If they are also holding the text, kids who struggle will read more slowly, getting caught up in hard words, losing meaning. Here, you read it aloud first, using your voice and gestures to add meaning. Then you might display part of it. If you have some kids who would benefit from prereading the text, gather those students first, and read the text aloud an extra time, in anticipation of the lesson.

To find arguments inside of topics, researchers ask...

What arguments or disputes come up inside of this topic?

What do people disagree about?

 What are some sides of these arguments?

 What groups or voices seem important in these debates?

Again, you're not hoping that kids will understand every word of this New York Times article—you're not doing a close shared reading here. You will do some close shared reading later in this bend. Here, you're inviting students to listen for the big disputes this article brings up. We suggest that if you do display the text now, it's after you've read a part aloud, and just display that part, and then move it off the screen and put your notebook up. Your notebook will serve as a scaffold for kids.

Then I invited kids to share their notes and thoughts with their research partners. After a minute, I interrupted them.

Compliment students on taking lean notes. Then explain that when a source mentions a prior case or event, especially a Supreme Court case, it's often worth noting as potentially crucial information. That is, their notes will need to become more specific in this bend.

"Readers, I noticed that you had a lot more to say to your partner than you wrote down. That has been a good move up to this point, to take lean notes, and pretty much always, you should have more to say than you've jotted. As you move forward in your research, though, your notes will need to become more specific. When you see a group mentioned more than once, that's worth noting, for example. That's why I jotted down this note about the ACLU.

"When you see a court case referenced—that's probably worth noting too. Supreme Court cases interpret the Constitution; we have to abide by those cases, so they're super important. So it's probably worth jotting down *Tinker* v. *Des Moines*."

Read on, inviting kids to continue to think about what's worth talking about and jotting down.

"Let's read on a bit, and as we do so, keep thinking about what kinds of disputes and arguments are arising. You may begin to see some sides here as well. Ready?"

I reread a sentence to reorient students, and then read on:

If you think some students need a little more support, retell the article so far before going on. Say something like, "Okay, so far the article has taught us about this kid called Bretton Barber. He wore a T-shirt to school, and the T-shirt called President Bush an international terrorist. His school sent Bretton home, and he's pretty sure that his constitutional rights were infringed. Bretton seems really well informed. He knows about the ACLU, which is a group that defends civil liberties, and he knows about a Supreme Court case called Tinker v Des Moines, *where a group of high school kids were allowed to wear antiwar arm bands. Okay, let's go on . . ."*

"When I asked why, he said I couldn't wear a shirt that promotes terrorism."

Mr. Barber is steeped in civil liberties law, so his talk with the principal, Judith Coebly, revolved around the *Tinker* case, which dealt with students who wore black armbands to protest the Vietnam War. In that case, the court found that students did "not shed their constitutional rights to freedom of speech or expression at the schoolhouse gate,'" although educators may stop expression that substantially interferes with the functioning of a school.

"She immediately asked if I was familiar with the Supreme Court case, *Tinker* v. *Des Moines*," Mr. Barber said. "I said I was very familiar with it. She said it happened in 1969. And I said no, it happened in 1965, but it got decided in 1969. Then she quoted directly from the dissenting opinion, to say that the school has the right to control speech. I knew that wasn't how the case came out, but I didn't argue with her."

High school officials were in meetings yesterday, and Ms. Coebly's office referred inquiries to a spokesman for the district, who did not return phone calls. Superintendent John G. Artis had previously said the schools had an obligation to maintain an environment "conducive to learning."

With the nation gearing up for war, Mr. Barber's T-shirt prompted reports in newspapers in many countries and rekindled the debate over students' rights to political expression. Although the Tinker case resolved the legal issue, as a practical matter, many school officials are quick to act when students express unpopular positions.

"Do some jotting. I will too." As students jotted, I added to my notes.

- Student v school administration
- The school thinks the school has the right to control speech.
- Tinker v Des Moines said students do have Constitutional right to free speech.
- Seems like the question is—does it disrupt education?

Give students an opportunity to talk; then explain how often, there are subtleties in these kinds of arguments. Researchers have to note conditions and context.

"Go ahead, talk to your partner. What were you struck by here?"

After a moment, I showed my notes. "Readers, as you're researching, you'll find that often, there are subtleties in these arguments. Like in this case, everyone agrees that the Constitution protects free speech, but not in every situation. It seems as if different Supreme Court cases have clarified some of those conditions where speech can be restricted. So, students have free speech, but not if it disrupts the school purpose of educating.

What do you think, would this T-shirt have disrupted that purpose? How much does it matter that it was a time of war?"

I gave students time with their research partners to discuss the points I raised.

Set kids up to listen to the end of the article, giving them lenses for how endings often either provide closure or raise new questions.

After a few minutes, I said, "Okay, let's read the last part of the article. Readers, articles that tackle these kinds of big arguments tend to end in one of two ways—either they wrap up with a sense of closure, answering some of the questions raised at the beginning—like in this case, can schools stop kids from political expression in school?—or they end by raising more questions. Let's see what kind of ending this is."

I reread two sentences, and then read on:

> With the nation gearing up for war, Mr. Barber's T-shirt prompted reports in newspapers in many countries and rekindled the debate over students' rights to political expression. Although the Tinker case resolved the legal issue, as a practical matter, many school officials are quick to act when students express unpopular positions.
>
> At Franklin D. Roosevelt High School on 20th Avenue in Bensonhurst, Brooklyn, Yusra Awadeh, 17, was taken from class in November, searched and told that she could not wear a T-shirt and pin that showed the Palestinian flag or display pro-Palestinian stickers. The school later reversed its decision.
>
> Education lawyers said it was not always clear what action an administrator might constitutionally take if a student wore clothing that expressed volatile views. The answer, the lawyers said, depends on factors like the history of the school and the composition of the student body.
>
> A spokeswoman for the Michigan chapter of the civil liberties union, Wendy Wagenheim, said, "Probably within the next week either the school will recognize that he has the right to express himself or we will seriously consider litigating."

"Hmm, . . . what do you think, did this answer all of our questions, or leave us with more? Go ahead, talk with your partner. What are you wondering about?"

I listened in, and then after a moment I summarized. "Readers, I can hear that this article is leaving you with questions about this dispute. You're wondering if the decision about political expression is made school by school, and whether that's fair. Some of you are wondering if it's okay for kids to wear political T-shirts that are popular, but not unpopular ones. You're wondering what you're allowed to wear and not wear right now,

Again, if you think it's needed, you can retell again, saying something like, "Let's summarize what we've learned so far, and then go on . . ." Then retell the most important points. You might say, "Bretton met with his principal, and she misremembered the important Supreme Court case, Tinker v. Des Moines. That case asserted that teens do have constitutional rights to free speech in school. Also, it's important to note that President Bush was gearing up to send U.S. troops to invade Iraq, so newspapers everywhere covered this story about a boy calling his president a terrorist. It was hot stuff."

if you're allowed to show support or criticize your current president in this school. These are huge questions. Take just a moment, and add anything crucial to your notes, including any of your questions—look back at our chart about what's worth jotting—is there anything else you should write down?"

As kids jotted, I did too.

- Are kids allowed to wear anti-president shirts to this school? Are teachers?
- How firm is <u>Tinker v Des Moines</u>? Who gets to decide if it's free speech or something else?

LINK

Send students off to meet with their study group to discuss any disputes or arguments that have come up so far. Suggest they make a plan to dive back into their research with a new lens.

"Researchers, the work you just did is important in two ways. One, you're getting a feel for how, inside of any important research topic, there will be arguments and disputes that are worth exploring. And two, you're becoming more aware of some of the legal history around free expression for teens, and that matters. Whatever topic you care about, you'll want to know a bit about how far your free speech is protected.

"You're going to have time to meet with your study group today, to figure out, together, any disputes or arguments that have come up so far in your research on your topic. Come up with a way to keep track of these. Then make a plan for diving back into your research, and do so. I'm guessing you'll want to return to texts that you read when you were building background knowledge, this time with a new lens, thinking about groups, sides, and perspectives, as well as possible pros and cons."

I started a new anchor chart.

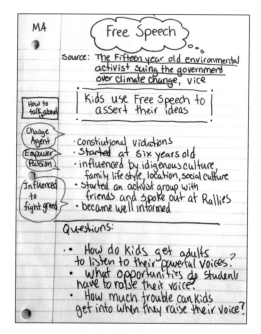

FIG. 9–1 Marc uses his own notebook as a demonstration text for jotting whle reading.

ANCHOR CHART

Ethical Researchers . . .

- Discern arguments and disputes inside of their research topic by . . .
  - returning to notes and texts
  - thinking about groups/sides/perspectives
  - wondering about pros and cons

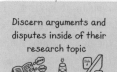

Discern arguments and disputes inside of their research topic

INDEPENDENT WORK

Teaching Teen Librarians to Curate Text Collections

As study groups go farther in their research, they'll want to add texts to their text collections—and you'll want to urge them to do so. It can be very helpful to inspire some kids to act as curators. It's helpful to you, because they can organize and add to the text collection of their study group. It's helpful to them, because a lot of intellectual kids are looking for peers and coaching and affirmation. And some kids may surprise you; there may be students who don't manifest as avid print readers, but they are very tech savvy, or they love the content they are studying.

You might nominate a student (or two) from each group, or ask students to volunteer. Then teach students how to annotate texts, either with a brief introduction at the top of the document in Google Docs, or with the same in a padlet, or by jotting Post-its on printed texts. Curators can also begin to categorize texts. They might annotate for level of difficulty, or for content, or for sides of an argument. Later in the unit, these students can lead peer conferences, teaching other students these same skills.

SHARE

Demonstrate how researchers narrow their focus to a more specific argument, one that has valid sides, that has support in the research text set, and that is interesting to the study group.

"I want to give you all an important tip. Which is, once researchers have gotten the lay of the land, they need to narrow their research focus. In your case, you'll want to focus on a specific part of a topic that you want to continue to research, knowing that you'll culminate all your information first into flash-debates, and later into a TED talk that promotes a position related to that focus.

"For instance, the topic of free speech is both too huge and too broad. But the focus 'Should students have free speech in school?' is narrower, and it's an interesting argument because both sides make valid points. And there are already lots of texts on free speech cases in schools, in our free speech text set. So sometimes, you find a more specific, interesting argument inside of your topic, and you can go forward with that focus.

"Or, you might find one focus inside of your topic disturbing—those kinds of focal points are often worth finding out more about. For instance, I was looking at an article about neo-Nazis marching. It's making me ask, 'Should even hate groups, like neo-Nazis, or white supremacists, groups that are violent and hate-filled, be able to say what they want?' So, maybe I want to look at restrictions in free speech related to hate speech."

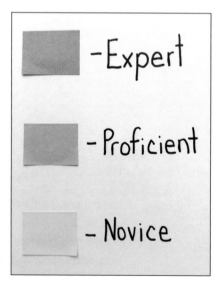

FIG. 9–2   Kids decide on a variety of systems, from difficulty level to background to specifics to subtopics.

Invite students to narrow their topics to a preliminary argument.

"Will you and your study group spend a few minutes now trying to narrow down your research topic to a preliminary argument you find interesting? It might be an argument that has two distinct sides, or groups supporting it, or it might be a dispute *inside* of one side of the argument." I showed a quick one-day chart "When researchers come up with debatable positions, they consider arguments that are . . ." to help students.

"An argument worth researching has to be specific, it has to involve differing legitimate points, it has to be relevant and interesting to you and your group, and it has to be researchable—one your texts have information about. When you know what you want to focus on within your broader topic, write it on one of these large Post-its, and stick it up on the wall, with your names. That way, if other groups or if I know of texts that might help you, we can leave you notes."

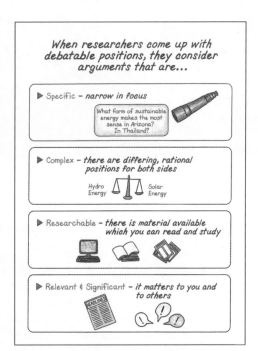

SESSION 9 HOMEWORK

REVIEWING YOUR TEXT SET TO REENERGIZE YOUR RESEARCH

Tomorrow, you'll dive back into your research, looking especially at the differing points of view you've found about your angle—for and against, for example. To prepare for that work, review the texts in your text set. Which ones would you like to return to first? Which ones do you remember taking up the focus you want to research? Be prepared to share this reading plan with a partner tomorrow.

Ethical Researchers Confront
Their Own Biases

✔ Get ready to display some images of rats on Google Images, some that are especially cute and some that are scary (see Teaching).

✔ Prepare images of movie characters that will help illustrate your own possible bias when it comes to free speech in schools (see Active Engagement).

✔ Be prepared to add to the "Ethical Researchers . . ." anchor chart (see Link).

IN THIS SESSION

TODAY you'll teach students that ethical researchers confront their own biases by considering their emotional attachment to the subject, and also their folk knowledge. These considerations help researchers determine the side of an argument they will have to research extra-fairly.

TODAY YOUR STUDENTS will learn to consider their own biases as they continue to research their topic. They will determine where their bias lies, and be especially careful to be fair to the side that they don't naturally support. They will return to texts they read in Bend 1, looking for evidence now of *both sides* of the argument they are researching. Study groups will meet today.

MINILESSON

CONNECTION

Alert students to a contemporary debate on rats, to lay the groundwork for how our own feelings can bias us in research.

"I want to engage you for a moment in a current debate. This issue has come up before tribunes in the United Nations, the Defense Department, the Centers for Disease Control, and the World Food Bank. The issue is . . . rats!

"It turns out that rats are incredibly useful for scientists who are studying diseases. They are also effective in finding unexploded landmines for the Defense Department and for militaries all over the world. Rats are a major food source in some places around the world. But rats also eat about 1/3 of the world's food each year, and rats spread disease, making epidemics possible. So a discussion that is current now, is: should rats be bred, farmed, and trained—or should we be trying to eradicate the rat population?

"Here's the thing, though. You probably have some pretty strong feelings about rats already. And those feelings could get in the way of your ability to do unbiased research."

❧ **Name the teaching point.**

"Today I want to teach you that ethical researchers confront their own biases. One way to do that is to consider your emotional attachment to the subject. Another way is to consider your folk knowledge—what you *think* you know. These considerations help researchers determine the side of an argument they will have to research extra-fairly."

TEACHING

Engage students in tackling their feelings about a sample topic, rats. Show some images and have students share their feelings about rats, as an example of one's emotional attachment to a topic.

"Let's try this together. Look at these images of rats. Tell your partner—what are your feelings about rats, in general. Like, if you opened your locker and saw one, would you think, how sweet, or yuck?"

I showed them a few images of rats, some cute and some terrifying.

"Go ahead, tell your partner. Do you like rats? Do you abhor them?"

After a minute, I said, "Researchers, what you're doing is thinking about what's called your *emotional attachment* to one side of an argument. Like, you may already love rats, or be afraid of them, or hate them. I could hear that some of you have very strong feelings about rats!"

Encourage students to reflect on where their feelings come from—the source of their folk knowledge.

"Let's take this one step farther. Think about where your feelings come from. Like, my feelings about sharks are deeply informed by making the terrible mistake of watching *Jaws* when I was your age. So even though I want to think sharks are amazing creatures, I also find them pretty terrifying and am sure they might want to kill me.

"So think for a moment. Where do your feelings about rats come from?"

Soon kids were talking about books and movies, subways, and pets.

"So interesting. Some of your feelings come from movies like *Ratatouille*. In those stories rats are heroes. But in other stories, like in the Harry Potter series, rats turn out to be sneaks, or they are cruel, like in *Charlotte's Web*. The main thing is, very few of you spoke about scientific research. This is super important. The kind of knowledge that comes from vague, hard-to-pinpoint but influential sources, is what scientists call folk knowledge—what you *think* you know about

If you have the time, it could be engaging to show images of famous rats to augment kids' discussions, from movies and pop culture. We've made a collection of these for the online resources. Visual cues help kids engage in dramatic ways. ✨

a topic. And it matters, because folk knowledge causes inadvertent bias. Like, I know rationally that great white sharks don't want to kill me. But still, those *Jaws* scenes haunt me."

Sum up the significance of acknowledging emotional attachment and folk knowledge, and of confronting the bias these may cause.

"There is a researcher named Jonathan Osbourne at Stanford University. He's done a lot of research on argument in science. His work shows how important it is to be alert to evidence for the side of an argument you don't already agree with. Ethical researchers confront their own biases, like we just did with rats. If you were to research rats, some of you would have to be extra careful to research the pro-rat side! Others of you would have to be careful to acknowledge anti-rat evidence fairly!"

ACTIVE ENGAGEMENT

Engage students in thinking about their own biases inside of the arguments they are researching. First demonstrate with your topic, free speech.

"Let's turn to our topics, now. I've decided to narrow my research to free speech in school. I tend to think that the whole purpose of school is to teach about democracy, and for kids to find their voices. So I already feel strongly that kids' voices should always be protected in school. Plus, I worry about adults oppressing kids. Now, I need to ask myself: Where do my feelings about kids being oppressed in school come from?"

I showed some quick stills from movies, including the principal from *Ferris Bueller's Day Off*; Richard Vernon, the antagonist in *The Breakfast Club*; and Dolores Umbridge from the Harry Potter series.

"I do feel strongly, but I'm realizing that some of these feelings may arise from fiction movies where adults abuse or torment kids in ways that are pretty over the top. So I need to think more about my source of knowledge, and I definitely need to be extra alert to evidence for the other side—that sometimes it may *not* be okay for kids to express themselves fully and openly in school."

Set partners up to discuss their possible biases, and the source of these biases. Then remind students of the significance of acknowledging their own biases as they research.

"Partners, give this a try. Think about the argument you are researching, and the sides of that argument. What side of that argument are you naturally sympathetic to? Where does that sympathy come from?"

I gave students some time to talk.

LINK

Ask students to make a research plan with a partner, and then send them back to their research, reminding them to be extra fair to the side of their argument they don't naturally agree with.

"As you go off to work today, researchers, will you have two things in mind? One is that you want to focus on rereading or reading parts of these texts that support both sides of the argument you are researching. And the other is you need to be especially careful to be fair to evidence for the side that you don't already support. You'll choose your own side soon, but you want to come to a considered opinion through ethical research.

"Today, you should spend about half an hour reading and taking notes. Take a moment to tell your partner your research plan. What text will you start with? How much do you hope to read today?"

After a minute I said, "I'll add this work to our anchor chart. As soon as you're ready, off you go. Try to find lots of evidence for both sides of your argument today."

FIG. 10–1 Olivia uses her notebook to explore pros and cons—working to research both sides of a topic.

ANCHOR CHART

Ethical Researchers . . .

- Discern arguments and disputes inside of their research topic by . . .
    - returning to notes and texts
    - thinking about groups/sides/perspectives
    - wondering about pros and cons
- **Research both sides of a topic fairly by . . .**
    - **acknowledging their emotional attachment to a side**
    - **considering their folk knowledge**
    - **being careful to research the opposite side extra fairly**

Research both sides
of a topic fairly

Finding Arguments that Are Sufficiently Relevant, Researchable, and Valid

SOME OF YOUR STUDENTS will need support finding arguments that are researchable, that are interesting to them, and that have valid sides. The following table shows some ideas for ways to support them.

Finding Arguments that Are Sufficiently Relevant, Researchable, and Valid	
If . . .	**Then . . .**
Students need support finding disputes and arguments in the bigger topic . . .	Teach students that controversies and arguments arise within all important issues because the people involved have so much at stake. You might make the following tool for their reference. One way to identify disputes is to ask yourself: • Who are the different groups involved in this issue? • What does each group want and why? • How might the interests of these groups collide? Ask students to write stakeholder groups on individual Post-its, then coach them into thinking about what each of these constituencies might want. Students can then sort the stakeholders into groups that might have similar interests and discuss how those interests might conflict with those of another group.
Students have chosen arguments with only one valid side . . .	You might teach them to stop stretching to look for an opposing argument and instead to look for disagreements *within* a chosen viewpoint. Disputes and disagreements don't always have to be between people on totally opposing sides. Sometimes people might have the same fundamental goal, but they have different opinions on how to achieve that goal. It often helps to think of superlatives like *best* and *most* when looking for arguments:

If . . .	Then . . .
	<ul><li>_____ thinks <u>the best way</u> to _____ is _____ whereas _____ thinks the best way to _____ is ____.</li><li>_____ thinks <u>the most effective</u> approach would be ____ while _____ thinks it would be more effective to ____.</li><li>_____ believes it is <u>most accurate</u> to say ____; on the other hand, ____ believes it is more accurate to say ____.</li></ul>
Students have chosen interesting arguments for which there are few texts available that the students can actually comprehend . . .	You'll need to coach students toward arguments that they can realistically read about, grasp, and analyze. If a student finds an interesting argument that is too technical or complex for them to research, you'll want to validate their interest while helping them see that it may have to be a research topic for later in their academic career. It often helps to point the student to a text that goes to the heart of their chosen issue and have them read it aloud to you. Ask the student to summarize the text and reflect on their comprehension. Often, students realize that what they've read may not be appropriate for them right now. Make sure that the student does not feel discouraged. You might say, "A curious and inquisitive researcher like you doesn't just find one possible researchable argument, they find several and they pick the one they have the resources to pursue."
Students have strong emotional attachments to an opinion and are having trouble recognizing valid alternatives . . .	You'll want to start by validating the student's strong opinion and their feelings about that opinion. Then, teach the student that ethical researchers do research not only with their heart, but also with their head. Explain that this can be hard to do, but that it's very important to try so that we don't blind ourselves to other possibilities that we never considered. You might invite students to try making an argument for the other side, and have them investigate if there are any shared concerns, beliefs, or goals between the two sides.
Students within a group feel that the group is stuck, especially in hearing everyone's voice . . .	Move toward student independence. Invite a student to call a quick "caucus" of fellow researchers to state the research problem and ask fellow researchers to share thoughts, texts, strategies, and/or notes. Follow a simple protocol: <ul><li>The student who called the caucus states the problem.</li><li>Each caucus member has one minute to share thoughts, texts, strategies, and/or notes.</li><li>Students who called the caucus will make clear "next steps plans."</li></ul>Then invite the group to try their discussion again, with heightened awareness of listening actively.

Refining and Revising Arguments to Be Even More Specific

Advise students that they'll often need to revise their argument focus, and demonstrate how you do this.

"Researchers, in a moment, I will ask you get back together with your study group, to share a bit of what you researched today. Be prepared to show your notes, and to see if you are fairly gathering evidence for both sides of the argument you are researching.

"As you do this work, be aware that you'll need to be open to refining and revising your argument as you research. You may find that you want to narrow your focus even more, that there is a *subtopic* that you are even more interested in. For example, I'm finding that I can focus even more within my first focus of free speech—education. I'm really interested in free speech and, more specifically, as it is related to high school.

"Or, you may find that the argument that you were considering taking up yesterday is also too general. Like, I will not argue that there are *never* conditions that justify limiting students' free speech. So I could refine my argument to something like":

> High school students' freedom of expression should be protected/limited while in school.

"As you get together with your study group, see what evidence you've gathered so far, and also think about refining your argument, and remaining open to that possibility across your research."

SESSION 10 HOMEWORK

RESEARCH ARGUMENTS

Today you began researching an argument inside your topic. Remember the skills you learned in the first bend of the unit, and make an independent group decision about what to do for homework. You'll share your work. Your choices include:

- reading or watching a text
- contributing to your study group (finding a new text, making a study tool)
- collecting vocabulary
- going back into your notes and adding annotations.

Studying Mentor Notebooks to Deepen and Personalize Note-Taking

Dear Colleagues,

We've put together collections of student notebooks and notebook pages to serve as mentors for your students. Of course, if you've got collections from prior students, use those or add those in. If you don't have them yet, you will soon! We've found that teachers and students get really inspired by seeing models. Here, we've put together some pages from some students' work in research studies including civics, social studies, and science.

We also videotaped some kids talking about their notebooks, including one pair of students who are curating exemplar notebook pages for their class. You'll find these images and videos in the online resources.

You'll find that we avoid prioritizing any one way of taking notes. We find Cornell notes somewhat inflexible, especially when an annotated diagram or flowchart would serve better. We don't think insisting on diagrams works best for all students or at all times. We think that researchers sometimes follow text structures when they take notes, sometimes they organize their notes according to the categories they are researching for a specific project, and often, they reorganize and reconceptualize along the way. We do love Nichole Carter's sketch notebooks, as we see students who hated note-taking come to love it. There's a link to her website, www.mrscarterhla.com, in the online resources. Most of the students' work you'll see here is inspired by other student work. The

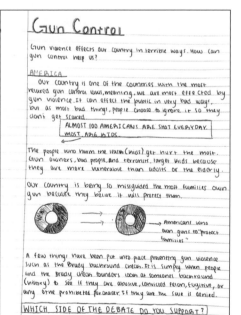

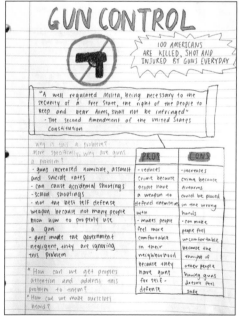

FIG. 11–1 When you study the work students do as note-takers, look for kids to show autonomy in their note-taking. Here, two study group members vary their structure.

83

main quality that runs through all of it is care—these researchers care about their notes—not in terms of neatness, but in terms of taking their notes seriously. ✳

You'll also see that there are some "long writes" that show students pausing to write about how their thinking has changed. This kind of reflective writing can really help students think about their thinking. We often give students time to do some of this writing in class—it makes for a good share, In five to ten minutes, most kids can write three-quarters of a page to a page, and it really helps them develop new thinking.

We do think it matters that you inspire your students to take notebooks seriously. Whether they use an iPad or a Moleskine, most students who do very well in higher-level classes in high school are working with their notes in serious ways. They go back in to redo their notes. They reorganize and annotate them. They create study guides and synthesis pages. They use color and tabs and all sorts of systems to help them consolidate their learning. All researchers who are going to publish take their notes seriously as well, because keeping track of sources, attending to quoting and paraphrasing, and referencing are serious issues for researchers. For some students, using a device will help them insert video or audio of themselves summarizing their thinking or showing their knowledge. Some of the apps for digital publishing also serve as a great platform for digital notebooks.

Today, we suggest that you set kids up in study groups and give them time to browse these mentor notes. They can flag pages they find interesting, and then talk with each other about these pages. You can either upload these images digitally, perhaps to Google classroom, or you can print them in color and put them in baskets or folders. Either way, kids will need some time to study and talk about the pages that they like. Encourage them, as well, to look at some of the notebook pages that show one student's work over time, to think about how that student's note-taking processes deepen.

Here's how you might set up this study: Give students a limited time (10–15 minutes) to study a variety of notebook mentors with the purpose of looking for ways to raise the level of their own notes. You might ask kids to stay in the meeting area, looking over sets of notes in groups of four or so; to take a gallery walk, where they circulate, studying sets of notes laid out on tables; or to stay within a study group.

You might pose an inquiry question such as this to guide kids' research of the mentor notes: How might this way of taking notes help a researcher to make use of the information later on?

As students work, you might prompt them to deepen their study, inviting them to notice the quality of the notes, what kinds of things are capturing their attention, what strategies they see being used, and what purpose those strategies might have. You might encourage students to take their own notes to capture their thinking as they research, perhaps setting their notes up in this way:

FIG. 11–2   Ask students if they'll lend their notebooks for next year's class. Soon, you and your colleagues will have a great collection that kids can study independently for inspiration.

Strategy	Purpose	Quality

Have students return to the meeting area and talk with their partner about what stood out to them. Have students name and record (or circle in their notes) one or two things they plan to try right away.

As students are working, it can be helpful for you to name some of what you see and admire. Be sure to admire student work that is thoughtful, but not necessarily neat handwriting, so that students realize it is the quality of thinking that matters.

You may find it helpful to either set study groups to documenting some of the ways of note-taking and qualities of notebook pages they find or pull the class back together and document this. If you jot as kids share, you'll end up with a chart that looks something like the "Thoughtful Note-Taking Strategies Include . . ." chart.

Students may also enjoy watching one or two of the videos of students talking about notebooks. You could make these available to study groups as well, and pose an inquiry question: what do these students value in terms of notes and notebooks?

Then you might give students time to think about their research so far, the texts they plan to read, and some of the ways they might take notes. Set up a time soon for a gallery walk of students' notebooks—not today, since they won't be prepared enough, but on a specific upcoming day. When students know that they'll be sharing one or two pages from their notebooks, they take their notebook work more seriously.

Kids can turn their notebook work around really quickly. Act as if they're going to love this, reinforce that it will help them with their academic studies, and then give them time to work. They'll surprise you. They surprise us, every time. It does help to have some swag around—gel pens, small Post-its, tabs, highlighters, colored pencils, and so on. And it helps if you let teachers across the disciplines know that your students are in an inquiry, where they are studying note-taking and notebooks. If students have the opportunity to take more independent notes in science, social studies, and English language arts, they really grow in independence and innovation.

For homework, have students set their own homework for research and note-taking, and tell them to be prepared to share their most recent research and note-taking on the following day, or a reflective long write. You'll use this work inside the minilesson in the following session.

All the best,
Mary and Marc

FIG. 11–3 Jaclyn shares another tool for colleagues and students.

Using a Continuum to Track the Fairness of Research

IN THIS SESSION

TODAY you'll teach students that researchers keep careful track of their sources. When researching multiple sides of an argument, they often keep track of sources along a continuum so they can assess the fairness of their research.

TODAY YOUR STUDENTS will first share the homework they set themselves. Then they'll practice tracking sources along a continuum by placing a source about free speech on a continuum. As they research today, they'll keep track of texts and sources along their own continuum. Study groups will not meet.

MINILESSON

CONNECTION

Invite students to share the homework they did last night. Notice which students are successful with setting and completing independent homework tasks, so you can support those who need it in conferences and small groups.

"Researchers, last night you set your own homework. Will you get out the work you did, and share it with your partner?"

As students did so, I circulated, noting kids who were beginning to do more significant homework, and kids who still needed support with this essential study habit.

"Researchers, I see that some of you found new sources for your study group last night, and some of you went back to sources that you had previewed while you were building background knowledge. Let's take a moment to think ahead now, to the flash-debate you'll give at the end of this bend, and to the more formal TED talk you'll give for our final unit celebration. When you give those talks, you'll want to refer to your sources not just by title or author, you'll also refer to what this source contributes to this argument."

❖ **Name the teaching point.**

"Today I want to teach you that researchers are careful to keep track of their sources. When researching multiple sides of an argument, it's often helpful to keep track of sources along a continuum that will allow you to assess the balance of sources in your research."

TEACHING

Demonstrate how you create and use a continuum to keep track of your sources for your demonstration argument on freedom of speech.

"Let me show you what this looks like. In our last session, I refined the position I'm researching to:"

High school students' freedom of expression should be protected yet limited while in school.

"So that means I could make a continuum that goes from one side of the argument to the other.

"I think that's my continuum. I was going to make it range from 'absolutely protected' to 'not protected' but yesterday I realized that really, the argument is 'mostly protected' versus 'limited.' I can always add 'not protected' to the continuum if I find some sources that argue that.

"Sometimes a text is arguing just one side of the argument, making it relatively easy to place on this continuum. I think I'll use blue Post-its for texts, and I'll put the Post-it toward one side or the other of the continuum depending on where I think that text falls.

"Now here is what's tricky. Most of the time, the texts I'm reading aren't making the same argument I am, or even necessarily making any argument. The texts are providing a lot of information. So what I'll have to do is really look inside the text, to see if any sources—groups, or people—may fall more on one side or the other of this continuum. I think I'll use green Post-its for people, or groups.

"Let's consider the article 'High School Tells Student to Remove Antiwar Shirt.' This is one of those informational texts, one that provides a lot of information, but doesn't take a side. Let's read through it and see if there are people or groups inside this text that seem strongly on one side or the other of this continuum." I displayed the text and skimmed, moving my finger down it, saying parts aloud.

"Okay, I'll try placing the student, Bretton Barber. It seems to me that Bretton Barber falls strongly on the 'free speech should be protected' side. Bretton wore a provocative T-shirt to school, one that criticized the president. And he did it knowingly. He quoted *Tinker v Des Moines*. He was willing to argue his case. He knows his case law, he is practicing freedom of expression, and he's an activist."

I made as if to put a green Post-it with *Bretton Barber* all the way to the far left of my continuum. Then I paused. "Though there is one thing—Bretton backed down when his principal misquoted *Tinker v Des Moines*—he didn't want to get in *too* much trouble. So I'm going to put him *almost* all the way over to the left."

I placed a green Post-it on which I had written *Bretton Barber* near the side of my continuum that said, "Should be absolutely protected."

Recap the steps you followed, reminding students that the text itself often won't explicitly fall on one side or the other of a continuum. Tell students they will need to read closely and infer.

"Readers, do you see how I wasn't expecting the text to just come out and say, 'This shows that Bretton was a strong defender of freedom of speech!' Instead, I had to think about the boy's actions and his words. I reread to think about evidence. Then I placed him on this continuum."

ACTIVE ENGAGEMENT

Engage students in practicing this work with another source inside this text, the principal, Ms. Coebly.

"Researchers, try this out with your partner. Where would you put Principal Coebly on this continuum—and why?"

FIG. 12–1 During Marc's read-aloud, as kids turn and talk, he moves in and listens to them.

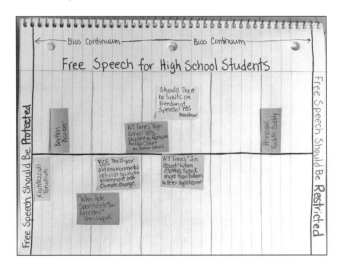

As students skimmed the article, I voiced over, "Think about her words as well as her actions."

Soon students were arguing to put Principal Coebly on the far right of the continuum, because she showed strong evidence through her actions and words that she felt students' free speech rights should be limited.

Give one more tip—it's important to note the original source—the text or video, so that researchers can find it and refer back to it, accurately, later on when writing, discussing, or presenting.

"Writers, I'm going to give you one important tip; when you defend your position in your flash-debates, and then later on, when you give your more formal TED talks, you're going to want to be able to refer to these sources accurately. An easy way to keep track of which articles or texts your sources come from is to write the name of the article on the back of these Post-its. If I do that, I'll be able to say something like, 'Bretton Barber, a high school student quoted in the *New York Times* article, "High School Tells Student to Remove Antiwar Shirt," is a strong advocate of protected free speech. He . . .'"

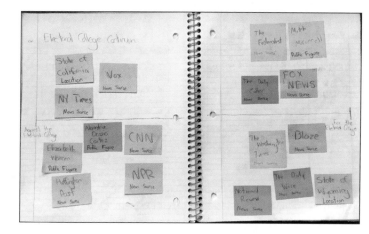

FIG. 12–2   The "voting rights" study group (Adam and Alan) keep meticulous track of the fairness of their research by starting a continuum in their notebook.

LINK

Send students off, clarifying how they'll incorporate this work into their research. Set expectations for volume of reading and note-taking.

"Before you begin your research today, start a continuum page in your notebook. You might take a moment to jot some Post-its for any texts or sources you've read that you can already place on this continuum. Then as you do new research, along with taking notes, keep track of resources along this continuum.

"Researchers, there is one logical consequence of this work. If you are noticing that most of your texts and sources are falling just along one side of your continuum, it will be important that you seek out resources for the other side. Ethical researchers want to make sure they are considering multiple points of view. It does not mean you have to take into account equal numbers on every side—sometimes you'll discover that there just isn't that much evidence to support one side or the other—but it's important to take note of the sources you are using, where they stand, and where your research stands.

"At some point, you can combine your research with that of your study group, and you'll have an incredible resource as you prepare for your TED talk. Off you go. You won't meet with study groups today, but you will get a chance to compare your research with a partner later. I expect most of you are going back into a second or third text today, and that you are probably on a second page of notes as well. You can use our anchor chart to remind you of the work you're doing." I added on to our anchor chart.

ANCHOR CHART

Ethical Researchers . . .

- Discern arguments and disputes inside of their research topic by . . .
  - returning to notes and texts
  - thinking about groups/sides/perspectives
  - wondering about pros and cons
- Research both sides of a topic fairly by . . .
  - acknowledging their emotional attachment to a side
  - considering their folk knowledge
  - being careful to research the opposite side extra fairly
- **Consider the fairness of their research often by . . .**
  - **using a continuum to keep track of texts and sources**
  - **considering what side of this continuum is more weighted**
  - **actively seeking sources along the continuum**

Consider the fairness of their research often

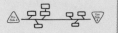

Supporting Students with Independence in Homework

I T IS CRUCIAL for students' academic success that they learn to do homework in middle and high school. It's even better for them if they learn to set their own study goals, on top of or in addition to class assignments. Remember our research—kids who do a bit more outside of school do better academically. This does not mean spending a lot more time—it means smart, strategic work, like finding an article or video, rereading or going over notes, or talking about the topic. Take time today to coach kids in this work. We've found these conversations go best in intimate, one-on-one conversations. Sometimes you can harness social bonds—use your judgment. Here are some examples of conversations you might have.

Supporting Students with Independence in Homework
Helping kids find time and space to do homework in very busy lives—and to advocate for themselves
There are many kids who are a lot like us; over-scheduled, overwhelmed, and sometimes desperate with all they need to do. They have soccer practice, or a game that keeps them on the field and bus until 9 pm. Their parents have scheduled a family event on a night when they have lots of homework. They have assignments due in four classes and don't know what to prioritize or even literally how to fit it all in. You'll want to listen hard to these kids. First, ask about their other homework, and their schedule across the week. Jot a little weekly calendar, and study it with them. Find out about their tasks, their commitments. Then help them to lay out a reasonable work plan. And show them how to help each other with this ongoing time management. You'll also need to teach students to advocate for themselves. They may need to ask teachers to share homework assignments earlier, so they have more time to plan across the week. Students may sometimes need to ask for extensions, and they will need help writing respectful emails to teachers; you can start by helping them write a draft to you, to keep as needed. The main thing is to bring all your wisdom to help these students with the ongoing, crucial task of managing academic, social, and work lives.

Helping kids care about their own work—increasing engagement and esteem

You may also have students who seem to care little or less about their work. They may seem withdrawn or uninterested. They may appear careless and uncaring. Remember that no kids come to school wanting to not achieve. Life is hard for lots of kids. There may be stuff going on in their families or their friendships. They may have huge issues that we know little about. They may be in the throes of adolescent anxiety about things that feel so big when you are that age. Adolescence can be a horrifying time, and kids often have little power or control over their lives.

For these kids, there are a couple of tips we suggest. The first is—don't back off, don't go away. Sometimes kids are waiting to see if you'll retreat. Keep showing them you care. The second is—don't get mad. Don't take their seeming lack of commitment personally. Stick with the message that you care about them learning to do homework, because you care about them.

Offer support in a variety of ways. You might open your classroom so kids can stay and do homework before they leave school, or when they arrive, or during lunch. You might help them find mentors—harness an older student, or another athlete for an athlete, or band member for band member. You might call home and say you see glimpses of this student's potential and you are eager to help him or her grow, and enlist family partners to encourage signs of interest or work.

Showing interested students how to do strategic additional work

Seek out students who seem especially interested in this class or in the topic. Remember to not only draw in students who are already intellectual powerhouses, but seek out the secret geeks, and the ones who are beginning to seem super interested. Sometimes you.can role-play kids into the academic identities you want for them.

Gather these kids, and remind them that research shows that kids who do even a little more outside of school end up doing very well academically. That little bit of extra work changes students' relationship with teachers. It changes their relationship with the content. And it can change their relationship with each other. You might engage these kids in listing a few things that can make a difference, in this study and in any class, such as:

- Visiting a museum or exhibition
- Talking to adults about the topic
- Reading and watching nonfiction around the topic
- Reading fiction and watching films around the topic
- Talking to other students

You're helping these kids build bonds with other students, you're helping then deepen their content knowledge and their study habits, and mostly, you're pointing them into an academic identity.

Addressing Fairness in Research

Advise partners to look over the continuum they each have made, to decide if they have sources from a broad enough set of stances.

"Researchers, when you meet with your partner to compare your research and the continuum you each made, will you look at where your Post-its are tending to fall? You should be able to see if your research has reached beyond a small segment of your continuum. It's tricky, because having *more* sources on a side doesn't mean those sources are more evidence-based. Still, an imbalance will alert you that you should talk with your group to see why it's like that, to see if you have more work to do.

"You'll end up on one side of this argument, but you want to make sure it's an informed position. Use your best judgment to decide if you have understood the different arguments and weighed them fairly, as you get closer to coming to your own considered position."

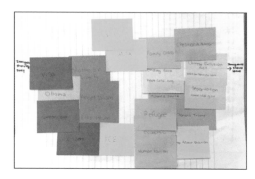

FIG. 12–3   This "immigration" study group innovates using a continuum to track groups, individuals, and forces.

SESSION 12 HOMEWORK

MAKING PLANS TO GROW YOUR BODY OF RESEARCH

Tonight, once again, set your own homework. Your choices include:

- reading or watching a text, adding the text or source information to your continuum, and taking some notes as or after you read

- contributing to your study group (finding a new text, making a study tool)

- collecting vocabulary

- going back into your notes and adding annotations

- writing long to reflect.

Studying Connotative Language for Implicit Text Bias

GETTING READY

✔ Have on hand the *New York Times* article from Session 9, "High School Tells Student to Remove Antiwar Shirt" (see Connection). ✷

✔ You'll share an excerpt from "In Court: When Clothes Speak to More Than Fashion" (see Teaching and Active Engagement). ✷

✔ Add on to the "Ethical Researchers . . ." anchor chart (see Link). ✷

✔ Be prepared to remind students of a tool from Session II (or introduce it here) on ways to choose note-taking strategies based on the structure of the text (see Conferring and Small-Group Work). ✷

IN THIS SESSION

TODAY you'll teach students that researchers know that even if a text doesn't seem biased, no text is ever truly neutral. Students can investigate the ways each text conveys a viewpoint on an argument by considering its connotative language—the way words are suggestive of people, events, and ideas. Often the word choice implies alignment with one side or point of view.

TODAY YOUR STUDENTS will continue their research, being alert to point of view and bias in text by paying attention to connotative language. At the end of the period, study groups will meet to compare their research and move closer to honing their own positions.

MINILESSON

CONNECTION

Share an anecdote that shows how two people might not retell an event in the same way.

"Researchers, I had this interesting experience yesterday. I was telling my friend Clayton about the *New York Times* article we had read, the one about the teenager who had worn a T-shirt critiquing the president. I hadn't even gotten to explain that we were talking about something that happened almost twenty years ago, so I think Clayton thought the kid had worn a shirt critiquing our current president. Then another friend joined us, and Clayton started to tell her what we were talking about.

"Here's what he said—see if you notice anything about the way he described what happened. He said, 'So, we're talking about this rebellious kid, who wore an outrageously inflammatory T-shirt to school, and it caused all kinds of disruption.'

"Tell your partner, what are you noticing about how Clayton described the event in the article?"

I listened in as kids talked about how Clayton seemed almost mad at the student, and how unsympathetic he seemed.

"I agree with what you're saying. Clayton's words, like *rebellious*, *inflammatory*, and *disruption*, all make it seem like he's not sympathetic to this kid. Whereas someone else might have said that this *courageous* kid *stood up for his rights* by wearing a *political T-shirt*, and that the principal *overreacted!*"

♣ **Name the teaching point.**

"Today I want to teach you that experienced researchers know that even if texts seem unbiased, they are never neutral. One way to investigate how a text may be more supportive of one side or another of an argument is to consider the connotative language—to consider associations with the words the author chooses in describing people, events, and ideas. Word choice often suggests sympathy to one side or the other."

TEACHING AND ACTIVE ENGAGEMENT

Engage students in a shared reading, studying any language that seems loaded. Make sure they have access to the text and can annotate it as you read.

"Readers, let's try this work. I've been reading a bunch of texts about kids struggling with free expression in school. I just read this *New York Times* article called 'In Court: When Clothes Speak to More Than Fashion.' It's by Peter Applebome." I handed a section of the text to students.

"Listen to this first paragraph. As I read it aloud, circle any words that suggest the author's point of view, even if it's not stated."

> *Given the importance placed on robust student expression, it's not completely surprising that a federal judge in New Jersey last week found himself opining on whether it was appropriate for two fifth-graders to be sporting buttons featuring Hitler Youth members. The occasion was a protest against the local school district's party-pooper policy mandating uniforms for students in kindergarten through the eighth grade.*

Give students a tip, namely that it is worth it to consider adjectives and verbs, because those often are suggestive of the sympathies of the author.

I let students work for a moment, then interrupted to give a tip. "Here's how I analyze language in this kind of text. I look for language that is surprising or very strongly worded. It's also often worth it to give an extra look at adjectives and verbs. The word choice for those can sometimes tell us something about the sympathies of the author."

Teachers, often our urge is to preteach strate-gies, and that can be very helpful, when you want students to try one strategy in particu-lar. But when you are working on a skill that involves multiple strategies it's also helpful to let students do a little work, so they are invested, and then add in a strategy as a tip. That's what you do here.

94

I showed the text I had marked up. "Let's compare."

Given the importance placed on <u>robust student expression</u>, it's not completely surprising that a federal judge in New Jersey last week found himself opining on whether it was appropriate for two fifth-graders to be <u>sporting</u> buttons featuring Hitler Youth members. The occasion was a protest against the local school district's <u>party-pooper</u> policy <u>mandating</u> uniforms for students in kindergarten through the eighth grade.

Demonstrate for students how to explain your annotations, knowing that sometimes your mind has intuitively recognized something that you need to seek words for; this is called transactional reading response.

"There is a great reading researcher named Louise Rosenblatt. She says that readers need to pay attention to their emotions as they read. So whenever you find something bothersome or surprising in a text, it's worth it to go back to that point, and explore what caught your attention.

"Let's try that here; let's go back to words that caught our attention, and try to analyze their significance. A lot of us underlined *robust student expression*. The adjective *robust* brings to mind health and strength, right? It seems complimentary, a word you'd choose if you tend to think students' expression should be healthy and strong.

"Then there is the verb *sporting*. The author doesn't say these fifth-graders were *flaunting*, or *aggressively displaying*, their buttons. Instead, he says they were *sporting* these buttons. Tell your partner, what images and associations does the word *sporting* suggest to you?"

I listened in, and then summarized. "I hear you saying that *sporting* seems playful and unthreatening, like healthy competition. So we get the impression that the author sympathizes with these students' actions. And then there is the *party-pooper* policy *mandating* uniforms! What associations do you have with those words?"

Give students a moment to discuss, and then restate your analysis, as well as the steps you followed to achieve it.

"So readers, we're coming to think that this author is sympathetic to these *robust* fifth-graders and their *sporting* actions and unsympathetic to the *party-pooper mandates* of the school.

"So while we noticed that the author never comes out and tells us that the school is wrong, and that we should side with the fifth-graders, we did notice some particularly strong or surprising language right away. We marked up the text, paying special attention especially to adjectives and verbs. Then we thought about the impact of that word choice. We analyzed that language for its potential connotations—how it suggested the sympathies of the author. This is important work that you will want to take back to your own research."

FIG. 13–1 Flexible seating helps kids find workplaces and develops more personal and independent study habits.

LINK

Send students off to work, reminding them that they want to get as much research done as possible. Let them know they can seek help with note-taking strategies if needed.

"Readers, you're not going to find any texts that are neutral; all text represents points of view, words have associations, always, language has a tone, always. But ethical readers can be alert to those points of view by paying attention to connotative, or loaded language, to word choice, to figures of speech and associations. I'll add this work to our anchor chart, to help us remember to check for that.

"You'll have a chance to meet with your study group later today. Until then, research as much as possible. You should be on your third or fourth text, at least, in researching your specific argument. Make sure that you are not only taking notes, but also keeping track of your texts (and maybe sources within your texts) along your continuum. I imagine you're also getting closer to figuring out your own position inside your argument.

"If you're struggling to take notes or don't love your notes, come see me, and we can work together to think about particular note-taking structures."

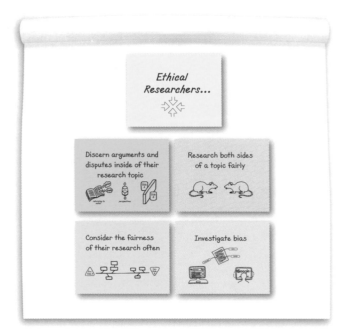

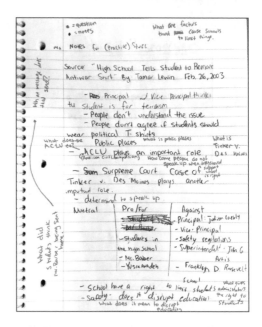

FIG. 13–2 Marc models how he annotates text and jots in his notebook. His notes are deliberately not hyper-neat or polished.

Using the Structure of the Text to Choose the Most Effective Note-Taking Strategy

LOTS OF STUDENTS imagine that when they are researching an argument, they will take notes only in a T-chart, or some structure that lets them capture the two sides of an argument. But more complex arguments will include research on things like court cases, historical events, speeches, and discoveries. That means it might make sense to sometimes make a timeline or flowchart. Or it might make sense to capture someone's ideas in boxes and bullets. Often, it's helpful for kids to learn how to follow the structure of the text (or part of the text), and use that structure to guide their note-taking strategy.

We've found a tool can be really helpful for kids, one that includes descriptions of some common text structures, and small graphics that show how those can link to particular note-taking strategies. We include a tool in the online resources that is essentially a chart offering different ways to take notes. This chart was first introduced in Session 11.

Powerful researchers use the structure of the text to choose the most effective note-taking strategy

If the text...	You might choose...	
· names some big ideas and supporting details	Boxes and Bullets	
· contains a lot of new or technical vocabulary	Vocabulary Tools	
· describes a process · cause and effect · problem → solution	Flowcharts	
· focuses on key events	Timeline	
· requires visualizing ideas as you read	Annotated Diagrams	
· shows connections between ideas	Concept Maps	
· compares ideas or describes parts of a larger idea	Charts	

Using the Structure of the Text to Choose the Most Effective Note-Taking Strategy	
If . . .	**Then . . .**
Students are taking notes from a hybrid text (one that includes different structures) . . .	You might coach students in previewing the text to consider how it is structured. A hybrid text might start with a narrative, and then move to more informational ideas and details, for instance. Show students how you consider varying your note-taking structure across the text.
Students are taking notes from a video . . .	Keep in mind that taking notes from a video can be a lot harder than taking notes from a print text. Often there is a narration, as well as visual imagery, as well as text boxes. Encourage students to preview the beginning of the text, to see how it seems to be organized. If the video isn't too long, it can be helpful to watch it through once, talk to a partner about the parts, and then go back to reread, taking notes the second time. Usually videos are hybrid in structure.
Students seem to keep choosing the same note-taking structure regardless of the type of text they are reading . . .	Check first to see if they have a way they are organizing their notes that fits with the parts of their argument. If so, that's beautiful—let them keep going. But chances are, they are using a note-taking strategy they learned at some point that they now feel comfortable with, and they are anxious about varying that strategy. For these students, it can be helpful to play the role of proficient partner, where you sit, look over the text with the student(s), and then discuss how the text is structured and what way of taking notes makes a lot of sense. Then help them get started— perhaps start a rough draft of a diagram, or boxes and bullets, and then leave them to it.
Students are ready to supersede the structure of the text for the structure of their argument when taking notes . . .	Coach these students to think about the parts or categories of their argument, so far. Then suggest that they might reorganize their notes, so that the notes they take are inside of these categories, or parts. For some students, taking notes on Post-its and then moving them around in their notebooks can be really helpful. For others, organizing pages for each part (they can always tape new pages in), and tucking new information in those parts, can work well.

Synthesizing Research Notes to Come to Preliminary Positions

Set students up to meet with their study groups. Let them know that as they synthesize their research, they also want to begin to come to a considered position, either as a group or as partnerships within the group.

"I'm sure you want some time now to meet with your study group. Before you meet, let me give you one tip. That is, as you compare and combine your research, remember that your overall goal is to come to a considered position inside this argument. So as you share, try to weigh and evaluate evidence, and think about what side of this argument you are beginning to support, based on the overall strength of evidence to support that side. And also think about what you'll want to acknowledge as valid points the other side makes.

"It may be that your whole group comes to one position. Or it may be that some of you differ, and you'll argue a different point of view within this argument."

SESSION 13 HOMEWORK

 RANKING EVIDENCE TO COME TO AN INITIAL POSITION

Tonight, review the research you and your study group have done so far. Figure out the strongest evidence for the position you are beginning to support. Be prepared to move forward in your research, with this preliminary position in mind—and be prepared to acknowledge convincing points for the other side. Tomorrow, you'll need to articulate the position you support, and why you support that position.

Investigating Authorship, Uncovering Agendas, and Critiquing Representation

GETTING READY

✔ Be prepared to show a snippet of the video "When Free Speech Gets You Arrested: A True Story about the Dangers of Handing Out the Constitution." A link to the video is available in the online resources (see Teaching).

✔ Students will need their research notebooks as well as the continuum of sources they began in Session 12. Research partners should sit together in the meeting area (see Active Engagement).

✔ Introduce a one-day chart, titled "Researchers find out more about the validity and reliability of their sources by . . . ," to guide students in researching the authors of their resources (see Active Engagement).

✔ Be prepared to add to the "Ethical Researchers . . ." anchor chart (see Link).

✔ Provide students with copies of the "Challenges Information Texts May Pose" and/or "Work Readers Do to Rise to the Challenges of Complexity" charts, as needed (see Conferring and Small-Group Work).

IN THIS SESSION

TODAY you'll teach students that researchers not only study content, but also authorship. Experienced researchers recognize that sometimes an author represents a group that may have agendas that are worth knowing about. Once researchers know more about an author, they can read more alertly, noticing when that author's agenda may express itself or when groups or people are represented in misleading or damaging ways.

TODAY YOUR STUDENTS will find out more about their sources to consider reliability and bias. They will continue their research to prepare for flash-debates at the end of the bend. Study groups will meet today.

MINILESSON

CONNECTION

Remind students of where they are in their research process, now getting ready for their flash-debates and eventually for TED talks in the next bend. Let them know that in any argument it is important to be able to reference not only evidence, but the source of that evidence.

"Researchers, in a few days you'll be testing your positions in flash-debates. And after that, you'll have time to prepare more finished TED talks in the next bend. At that time, it's going to be important that you not only have lots of evidence to support your cause, but that you've also fairly acknowledged evidence for other points of view. I want to remind you that it's going to be important that you know something about the source of that evidence. That is what gives your research, your argument too, authority.

"For instance, imagine in my argument I want to refer to the kid who wore that T-shirt to school—remember, from that article 'High School Tells Student to Remove Antiwar Shirt'? Rather than just saying something like, 'Once a teenager in Michigan wore a political shirt to school,' my position is more credible if I say something like, 'In a case that became famous when it was reported in the *New York Times* in 2003, a teenager in Michigan wore . . .'

"There is more to this, though, than simply acknowledging expertise and authority of sources. Sometimes, when you are experiencing a text, you begin to feel that you, or groups of people, aren't represented fairly in the text. When that happens, pay attention to that feeling. Louise Rosenblatt, an important researcher in reading, says to pay attention when your emotions are triggered by a text. Chances are, something is going on in the text that deserves investigating.

"But here's the thing—you already know how to study the language of the text. Sometimes, you have to go beyond that, to study the author as well."

❖ **Name the teaching point.**

"Today I want to teach you that researchers not only study content, they also find out more about authors. Sometimes an author represents a group that has agendas that are worth knowing about. Then researchers keep that agenda in mind as they critically consider the author's language and content, including how people and groups are represented in the text."

TEACHING

Show students a snippet of a text that at first seems innocuous, but upon research represents a group with a hidden agenda. Invite students to talk about its tone.

"Let me show you what I mean. I was researching free speech as related to students, and I came across what seemed like a pretty innocuous video: 'When Free Speech Gets You Arrested.' Let me show you just the first few minutes of this text."

I played just the first minute and half of the text (to 1:30) and invited kids to talk about its tone. "Go ahead, talk to your partner. What do you notice about its tone? And remember what you've learned about connotative language."

Explain how you try to pay attention to connotative language while reviewing the text. Then show how you also research the author.

"So, I'm honestly not sure exactly what made me feel uneasy here. There was something about the author's tone and language that seemed off. So then I went back and tried to pay more attention to this text's connotative language.

"It's describing these three teens: Michelle, Nathan, and Isaac. They 'work hard, they study, and they hang out with their friends.' And then the video says, 'But Michelle, Nathan, and Isaac aren't ordinary people. Because ordinary people haven't been arrested and hauled off to jail.' Friends, what does that mean, 'ordinary people aren't hauled off to jail'? It's a weird statement, I thought, because *breaking the law* is the first thing I think about when I think of getting hauled off to jail—whether you are 'ordinary' or not. And then I got to thinking, what do they even mean, *ordinary* people? They don't mean *not famous* . . . they seem to mean *good people* don't get arrested.

"It's so subtle, isn't it? But it's worth thinking about whether this representation is fair. Because of course, a lot of important and good people *have* been arrested. Nelson Mandela. Dr. Martin Luther King. Rosa Parks. A lot of good, ordinary people were arrested for civil disobedience during the civil rights movement. And sometimes students have been arrested for being in the wrong place at the wrong time, or making a youthful mistake, or someone makes a mistake about them! But this group suggests that only nonordinary people are ever arrested. Hmm, . . . not true.

"So, that uneasiness about how people were represented prompted me to do more research about the group.

"It turns out that they are a group that has agendas other than promoting free speech. One of these agendas is promoting arrests and/or criminalization of activities of LGBTQ citizens and undocumented immigrants. That surprised me, since I wasn't expecting that agenda to relate to free speech! So maybe, when I noticed something odd, or nonsensical in the video—this bit about *ordinary* people and how they act and how they never get arrested—I was getting a hint of this group's other agendas. Agendas about who is 'ordinary' in their definition and who is not, and how for this group, 'ordinary' is code for 'good.' That agenda informs how they frame this text about free speech, so I need to know that as I decide how to *read* their video."

Let students know that all authors merit research, to check for validity, reliability, and possible bias.

"Readers, we need to be alert to unfair or biased representations, and to information passed along to us without evidence. Even subtle messages like this one, passed along to us unchecked! One way to do that is to research the authors of the resources. Then it may be easier to spot ways they might try to influence us without evidence. That will help you check the validity of the sources you include, and it will help you read alert to other agendas in those sources."

ACTIVE ENGAGEMENT

Give students a chance to study their own authors, and offer a tool to help them find out more about them.

"Let's give you a chance to try this out. You have your continuum, where you've placed the texts, and some sources in them, that you've been researching. Will you get that out, and will you study it with your partner? Which of these authors and publishers do you know anything about? Do they have public agendas? How might you find out more about them?" I gave students a few minutes to talk, and then introduced a small chart to support their work.

"Researchers, there are a few ways to go about finding out more about your authors. Here's a chart of strategies that might help you. Will you look at it and decide with your partner on a strategy or two that you might try?"

Soon students were planning which texts they might investigate more, and how they might find out more about authors and groups.

LINK

Let students know that we all succumb to bias at times, and that what we strive for is to be as responsible as possible in our references.

"Readers, it's impossible that you will never, ever, quote someone whom later you wish you hadn't. You'll think, 'I didn't know that was a biased group. How could I not know that?' Or you'll find out that someone you quoted is known for his or her extremist position. Life, and texts, are full of things we don't know, and we'll find ourselves making mistakes along the way.

"But what you *can* do is strive to be responsible, to find out more about your sources, to consider evidence and bias. You can look into the history of different groups and organizations, so that you are more aware. And you can read differently, knowing that some texts aim to recruit you to their cause, or to pull you into agendas.

"Will you take a moment with your partner and look at our anchor chart? Make a plan for the work you'll do today, knowing that you want to move your research forward in smart and ethical ways. Will you go back and research authors of texts you've already taken notes on? Will you read new texts, but with a new awareness of authorship and a new alertness to representation? Are you ready to annotate or synthesize parts of your notes? You have lots of choices! Make a quick plan, and off you go."

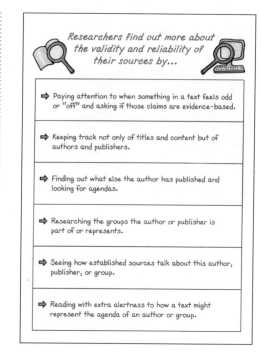

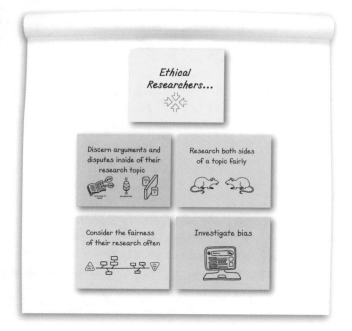

Strategies for Tackling Text Complexity

THERE ARE A VARIETY OF WAYS that the texts students are reading may pose challenges for them, whether these texts are print or digital, articles or videos. Rather than teaching kids one strategy at a time, we suggest that you might put a tool in their hands, to help them assess the challenges of some of their texts, and to help them come up with possible responses to these challenges.

Here are a variety of ways we've seen teachers and students use this tool to enable students to tackle text complexity more independently and effectively.

1. Give students the entire first page—"Challenges Information Texts May Pose"—and invite them to lay it alongside one of their more challenging texts. Then invite them to play a kind of "text-complexity" bingo, where they put a small Post-it over any of the squares that describe a challenge this text poses. Then hand them the second page—"Work Readers Do to Rise to Challenges of Complexity—and suggest that they again play a kind of readers' bingo where they mark any strategies they've tried so far. Often, kids find that they've tried a few strategies, and they come up with new ideas for reading work they can try. Other times, they *say* they tried a strategy, but when you suggest they choose one or two to return to, they really go off and try it for the first time.

2. Cut the "Challenges Information Texts May Pose" page into separate squares, and put these in a baggie, along with a glue stick and Post-its. Invite students to Post-it parts of the text where they encountered a particular text-complexity challenge. Offer students another baggie, with the page "Work Readers Do to Rise to Challenges of Complexity" also cut into squares, and have them work with a partner to try to match a strategy, or more than one strategy, to a challenge. Then have them rank the challenges and strategies that they think will most help their reading work.

3. For the most support, you can copy the two pages double-sided, so the strategy matches the challenge, and cut the page into squares. Then you can have students rank the challenges, choosing just the most common one or two. Have them find places in the text where that challenge arises. Then have them turn over the square to find a strategy to apply.

4. Invite students to add to these tools. We suggest a challenge of "The text is digital and complicated to follow." Possible strategies to deal with this challenge could be:

    - previewing the parts
    - making a reading plan
    - considering hyperlinks
    - navigating back to the original text.

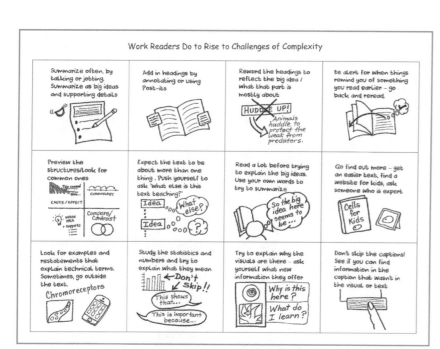

Work Readers Do to Rise to Challenges of Complexity

Summarize often, by talking or jotting. Summarize as big ideas and supporting details	Add in headings by annotating or using Post-its	Reword the headings to reflect the big idea / what that part is mostly about	Be alert for when things remind you of something you read earlier – go back and reread
Preview the structures/Look for common ones	Expect the text to be about more than one thing. Push yourself to ask 'what else is this text teaching?'	Read a lot before trying to explain the big idea. Use your own words to try to summarize	Go find out more – get an easier text, find a website for kids, ask someone who is expert
Look for examples and restatements that explain technical terms. Sometimes, go outside the text.	Study the statistics and numbers and try to explain what they mean	Try to explain why the visuals are there – ask yourself what new information they offer	Don't skip the captions! See if you can find information in the caption that wasn't in the visual or text

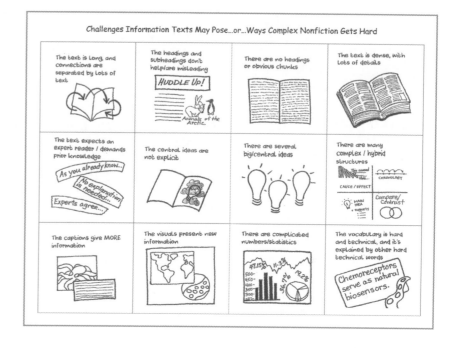

Challenges Information Texts May Pose...or...Ways Complex Nonfiction Gets Hard

The text is long, and connections are separated by lots of text	The headings and subheadings don't help/are misleading	There are no headings or obvious chunks	The text is dense, with lots of details
The text expects an expert reader / demands prior knowledge	The central ideas are not explicit	There are several big/central ideas	There are many complex / hybrid structures
The captions give MORE information	The visuals present new information	There are complicated numbers/statistics	The vocabulary is hard and technical, and it's explained by other hard technical words

Free-Writing to Respond to Issues of Representation

Set students up to write long in response to representation in the texts they've encountered, including dealing with how they, personally, and other people and groups are represented.

"Researchers, sometimes when you are researching, it's not just your intellect that is activated. Your emotions are too. You are an unusually ethical group of researchers. You care about who is left out in the texts you read, and whose representation may be unfair or distorted. Here's what I suggest for figuring out how you think and feel about issues of representation in the texts you've been reading. I suggest free-writing—writing fast and long, getting words down on the page about what you're thinking and what you're feeling.

"Let's try that now. Open up your notebook to a new page. Think about what feels fair and unfair, what kinds of people and groups have been represented a lot in your texts and which not so much. Think about how *you* are represented or ignored in these texts. And write what it makes you think and feel."

SESSION 14 HOMEWORK

MAKING HOMEWORK PLANS OVER TIME AND MOVING YOUR WORK FORWARD ACCORDING TO PLANS

Often, in high school and definitely in college, you don't have homework set for you each night. Instead, you have due dates, drafts, and projects. That means that you have to get good at looking at your own calendar and schedule and figuring out what nights or days you can get a lot of work done and when you really can't. Like, for some of you, the weekend is a great time to catch up on or get ahead of work but for others, it's not at all.

Assume that you want to do some work to move your research and thinking forward and to support the work of your study group outside of school. That could mean going on with the long writing you started in class. It could mean going back into your notes to annotate. It could mean something bigger, like making a synthesis page or infographic. It could mean reading or watching a new text. Look across your week and talk about which nights you can do bigger work for this and what nights you need to do leaner work. Then, plan that work. Keep in mind that, in a few days, you'll be participating in flash-debates to rehearse your argument, and that in about a week, you'll be giving TED Talks. Work accordingly.

The Non-Neutrality of Search Engines

IN THIS SESSION

TODAY you'll teach students that search engines aren't neutral; all use of the Internet results in the researcher being researched. You'll alert students to how search engine results are often biased toward past searches and the results can lead to confirmation bias.

TODAY YOUR STUDENTS will learn about the "echo chamber" effect and consider how to resist this kind of confirmation bias as they wrap up their research. Study groups will not meet today.

GETTING READY

✔ Prepare to show an image from the video, "When Free Speech Gets You Arrested." A link to the video is available in the online resources (see Teaching).

✔ Prepare to display the news app Blue Feed, Red Feed. A link to this app is available in the online resources (see Active Engagement).

✔ Be prepared to create a chart, "Striving to avoid the 'Echo Chamber'." We've provided Marc's sample and a digital version (see Active Engagement).

✔ Add on to the "Ethical Researchers . . ." anchor chart (see Link).

MINILESSON

CONNECTION

Tell a story about following a pop star on the Internet, and finding yourself inundated with more information every time you open your computer. Then invite students to share similar stories.

"Researchers, I want to share with you something that is sort of funny. I have these two friends, Kate and Maggie, and they were, for a long time, very into Justin Bieber. These are two very smart and funny and influential women, and so soon, all our friends were into Justin Bieber, too. We followed what was going on with him, we played his music at work, we would watch his new videos together.

"So here's what happened. After a while, every time I would turn on my computer, I would get these emails saying that Justin had a new song out. Or I would open the news, and the top story for me would be what Justin had recently done! It was kind of embarrassing. I mean, Justin Bieber appeared all over my computer, every day.

"Have you ever had anything like that happen? Where you were watching videos or looking up songs, or following somebody online, and then you'd get alerts and badges and banners and stuff about them? Turn and tell your partner."

I listened in and then recapped.

"Your stories are better than mine! Some of you follow Jay-Z and you hear about new songs. Some of you follow Lionel Messi, and you get alerts about his injuries and recoveries. Some of you have a favorite soccer team, and you hear all about every player. Some of you have other heroes. What's important here is that every time you use your computer to learn more about these people, the Internet is also learning more about you."

❖ Name the teaching point.

"Researchers, I want to alert you to something in the research process that is rather hidden. That is, search engines aren't neutral. Every time you use the Internet, every time you click on something, that information is used to shape what is offered to you the next time."

TEACHING

Describe how a search engine is affected by the texts you choose to open, so that future searches give you other similar results.

"With the Justin Bieber research, it was just annoying. But with real research you are doing, this can be serious. Do you remember how I spent time researching a text before I realized that it was published by what turned out to be a group that was anti-immigration and anti-LGBTQ? It was that video, 'When Free Speech Gets You Arrested,' that was put out by the Alliance Defending Freedom."

FIG. 15–1 Kids can share devices when doing digital research—a good lesson on sharing resources.

I pulled up an image of the video as a reminder.

"I haven't opened any other texts by them. But I *had* watched the video three or four times before I realized the agendas of the group. Well, imagine my surprise: every time I went to search 'free speech' on Google, I keep getting results that linked to this group, or to other groups with similar agendas!

"Finally, I tried something with a colleague. We both put the same search terms into our search engine, Google. We entered 'free speech teens school.' And we got different results. Because I had spent time in a site with a specific agenda, my search engine gave me a lot of results published by groups with the same agendas. My colleague hadn't, and she got different results!"

ACTIVE ENGAGEMENT

Engage students in studying an example of the echo chamber effect—how the texts we encounter can be restricted by our past searches or biases—perhaps using the news app Blue Feed, Red Feed.

"When you dig into how the Internet is studying you, you learn that whatever bias we have, it's going to be 'fed,' because our search engines are going to keep giving us results it assumes—from our research history—that we are looking for. Media scholars are calling this effect an 'echo chamber,' where pretty soon, people only hear back their own ideas and opinions, just like an echo.

"Let's try making some of this more visible."

I opened the news app Blue Feed, Red Feed and gave students an opportunity to read the history and purpose of the app. "I see you are getting the idea. One news event, but people with 'red politics' are fed online versions one way. People with search histories that are more 'blue politic' are fed online versions of the same event that are different. Let's look a bit more closely with an example news event that we choose." I chose a topic with them that I had previewed earlier to make sure it was appropriate.

"With a partner, talk about what you notice about the difference in the headlines, the photos, the tone. What is highlighted in each version?"

Soon students were noticing the tone that was for or against the current issue, with strong connotative language on both sides, and the use of images to stir up emotions.

"It's interesting, right? Can you see how different the tone is on these sites? And how easy it would be to slip into that echo chamber, where if you weren't careful, you would only encounter articles and videos that confirmed the ideas you already had? And that wouldn't be very fair or ethical or interesting research."

Engage students in considering how to resist the echo chamber effect of search-engine-learned bias.

"So, the questions we have to ask are: What can we do about this? How can we avoid the echo chamber effect? Talk to your partner—what ideas do you have?" As students talked, I charted some of their ideas.

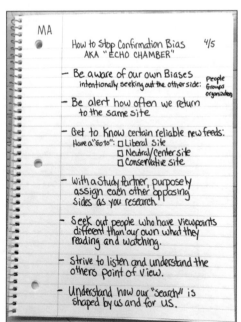

Teachers, you want to open any site before you show it to students. Blue Feed, Red Feed has a variety of subtopics you can demonstrate with—and it's real-time news, so you need to preview! On one day when we wanted to show this site, the immigration topic was perfect for this demonstration—it showed very different perspectives, and the articles, while angled, weren't inappropriate. On another day, the headlines weren't right for a classroom. So as with all Internet use in classrooms, do preview, and use your judgment. The truth is, our students encounter unfiltered media every day, and our goal here is to help them become better at filtering for themselves. But you don't want to show more than you intended!

As you create a chart with students, even if you have it mostly prepared ahead of time, you can make them feel like they coauthored it.

LINK

Remind students that they'll have time to work on their flash-debates tomorrow, and set them up for final research today.

"Researchers, these are some smart moves. You have about one more day to do some final research before your flash-debates. As you set out to do this, will you take your own advice, and try one of these strategies, to avoid the echo chamber?

"Make a quick plan with your research partner. Assuming you have one more day to do research, and you want to both have the strongest evidence to support your position and also be fair to the other side, what do you want to find out more about? How might you do that?"

I waited a moment then said, "I'll add this tip to our anchor chart. Use it as a reminder, and off you go. You won't meet with your study group today, but will tomorrow, to begin to plan and rehearse your flash-debates."

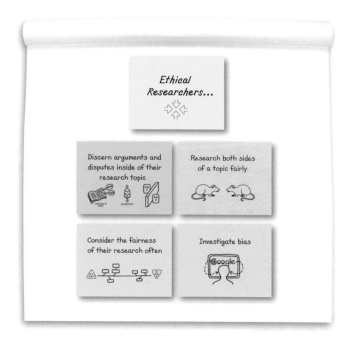

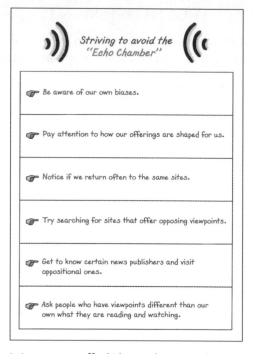

Later, you can offer kids a tool or mini-chart as a reminder.

Checking in on Transference

YOU HAVE ASKED A LOT OF STUDENTS in this unit so far; we all know these topics of truth and news and reliability in the age of the Internet and social-media-as-news-platforms are highly complex! These topics are in many ways new to our world of reading and researching; they add new requirements and layer new skills to what is essential to being a good reader—for us as adults as well as for our teens. We are learning ways to be responsible readers and learners afresh, as a society in this age. Because of the complexity and importance of the work, we recommend you take today's conferring time to check in with partnerships, groups, or even individuals about how they are doing writ large with this work.

First, yes, you might check in on if they've understood the teaching points lately, and to do so you might see if they've transferred them well to their work on their own research project. You might ask:

- In your research, exactly what kind of links is Google or YouTube prioritizing for you, now, do you think? What topics and points of view are your search results likely to be, mostly?

- What kind of links do you think you might be missing? Do you have questions about your own point of view?

- What exactly could you do to find some of what you might be missing? (Use the anchor chart to remind you, if you need to.)

But perhaps more importantly, you might take this time to confer with them about the import of these recent teaching points on *all* their reading and research, not just this project, and in fact, on all their life. If students seem to have understood these teaching points well and have begun applying them to their current work, this could be the perfect time to help them reflect on the larger role the Internet's algorithms may play in their lives. You could even help them transfer their learning about the process for detecting a text's viewpoint or bias onto other content areas or readings. You might initiate conversations like these:

- Have you thought about how all texts are biased—all texts have a point of view—before these lessons? Have you noticed it more since we started talking about it? How has that been going?

- Have you looked for points of view in more of your reading, even in other subjects since we started this unit? The process is the same as what we've applied here; what would you do first if you were going to look for bias in your textbook?

- Have you ever thought about finding the points of view or bias toward a topic or issue in the fiction you read? Certainly you already know that characters in your books have points of view, but also, narrators in books, or the voice in which books are told, have points of view. Have you ever looked for that? It's the same process, pretty much: first you think of an issue that is part of the story, then you look at how it's written about—what are the associations brought to it, and what, overall, does the book convey about that topic?

- Have you looked at information that comes to you through social media differently since we started this unit? How? How might you do something differently because of what we've learned?

- Have you thought about how ads online differ according to each person's search history? How might that impact you and what might you do differently now that you know it happens?

No matter how you approach it, we recommend giving your students some conversational space to process with you what they are learning about how the online world of information works. Encourage them to make connections between their ideas about this project and to their ideas about research and learning in general. Support them in making plans—nearly any plans at all—to be strategic rather than passive in their information consumption and search engine use. All in all, offer them some time, mental space, and some tips of support for inventing and reinventing themselves as readers in this, the Age of Information.

Confronting Confirmation Bias

Alert students to how their own bias can impact their openness to new ideas or information that may conflict with what they already believe.

"Researchers, we started today by studying how search engines aren't neutral. Well, we aren't neutral either. Everybody tends to slip into what's called confirmation bias. That's when we are more open to ideas and information that fit with the opinions we already have, and we tend to reject or ignore stuff that doesn't confirm our own ideas.

"Will you talk with your partner about parts of your topic that you may have to be more wary of your confirmation bias? Usually, it's any part that you feel very strongly about. And what can you do to resist that confirmation bias?"

Soon students were talking about the things they felt very strongly about.

"Tonight, look back over your notes. See what you might do, either color-coding or annotating, to show what research has confirmed your own sympathies, and what has taught you something new or interrupted your thinking."

SESSION 15 HOMEWORK

 ## REVISITING NOTES TO GROW YOUR THINKING ABOUT BIAS

Tonight, look back over your notes. See what you might do, either by color-coding or annotating, to show what research has confirmed your own sympathies, and what has taught you something new or interrupted your thinking. Do any annotating to show how you are thinking about confirmation bias.

Remaining Alert to the Possibilities of Fake News

IN THIS SESSION

TODAY you'll teach students that researchers can use protocols to assess whether a text is fake news and may be fabricated or distorted.

TODAY YOUR STUDENTS will continue their research as well as reconsider whether a text contains fake news, by comparing it to other texts that refer to the same topic or events. They will look back over their cumulative research and fill any gaps that may remain, in preparation for their upcoming flash-debates.

GETTING READY

✔ Prepare a chart titled "The 5 Ws and an H Protocol" (see Teaching).

✔ Students should sit with their research partners in the meeting area (see Active Engagement).

✔ Add on to the "Ethical Researchers . . ." anchor chart (see Link).

MINILESSON

CONNECTION

Tell a brief anecdote about being reminded to check for fake news.

"Researchers, I have to admit something to you. Remember how I had been lured into that video, 'When Free Speech Gets You Arrested,' and that since I watched it several times, I was constantly being shown more websites like it?

"Well, I was describing the video to a high school student, Jackson, and the first thing he asked was, 'Did you check if it's fake news?'

"I was so embarrassed. Here I am, a teacher, and it hadn't occurred to me to check that first—and it was the first thing this high school student thought! It really made me think about how all of us, your generation too, have to be such critical consumers of media, because there is such a huge volume of misinformation out there."

🍀 **Name the teaching point.**

"Researchers, today I want to teach you that when you have a feeling that something about a text might be off—and sometimes even if you don't have that feeling—you'll want to check if the text may be fake news. That is, it may be made up to attack someone or some cause, or it may be distorted, and you'll want to use a protocol to check to see if the facts of it are correct."

TEACHING

Teach students a protocol for investigating possible fake news. Refer to the "5Ws and an H" that journalists often use when writing investigative pieces. Then explain how to use this protocol to consider what parts of a piece are well documented, and what parts are not.

"One way to go about this work, researchers, is to apply a protocol. I want to share with you a protocol that journalists often use when they are writing, and it can help us as readers. That is, to think about a text analytically, you can ask about what journalists call the 5Ws and an H." I showed a small chart.

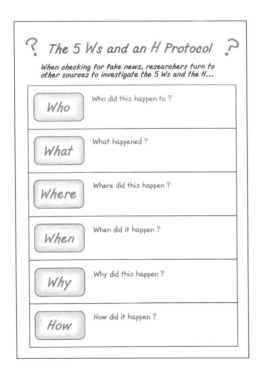

FIG. 16–1 Technology can be a tremendous instructional asset. We love the combination of a document camera and some kind of Smart Board or Apple TV to show student work, real-time work, videos, and websites.

"First, you need to figure out what details the original text offers for these 5Ws and the H. Notice if anything seems vague, as vague facts are often a marker of fake news. Then, you have to go to other texts, and compare references, remembering what we said about some news sites and groups being established. What's tricky is that some news sites aren't investigative—they're called news aggregators, and they simply re-post from other sites. So that means we need to find articles or news sites that refer to these same events, and then we need to compare what they say with the text we are assessing for authenticity."

Show students how you study the results of this investigation. Show a table with research on the first part of the 5Ws and the H.

"I followed the 5Ws and an H protocol to investigate the authenticity of the 'When Free Speech Gets You Arrested' video and did some of that research. I asked friends to help as well, and here is the first part of these results. We turned to news media that have a public presence or that are followed up locally. Will you study these notes with a partner, and talk through what you notice? If you're interested, you can visit the sites later."

After students talk, point out that fake news often has a kernel of truth that has been distorted. Point to those distortions here. Then remind students of the analytical steps you've followed.

"It's so interesting, because there is some truth in the story in the video. These students were at Kellogg Community College, that is not to be disputed. But it turns out that it's not clear that Michelle and Isaac were KCC students. It looks like they were not enrolled at that time. They had come over to KCC from their own universities—in fact, Isaac was an activist for Young Americans for Liberty at Michigan State.

"Researchers, do you see how I went to a variety of other sources, being careful that these sources weren't just reposting the video I had watched. And I jotted down the 5Ws and an H, and started to look for discrepancies. As I did so, I was alert to when something had been distorted, since often fake news doesn't totally invent, it starts with a kernel of truth that it then distorts or exaggerates or adds some falsehoods to the truth. I would want to check things out even more, but clearly things are more muddled than this video portrayed."

ACTIVE ENGAGEMENT

Engage students in continuing to analyze research results for the 5Ws and an H for the "When Free Speech Gets You Arrested" video. Provide them with copies of your research table.

"Researchers, will you see what else you notice when you study the rest of the 5Ws and an H that I investigated? Look this over with a partner."

I displayed my notes.

Soon students were pointing to discrepancies, talking about the distinctions between these sources.

FIG. 16–2 Marc demonstrates how to keep track of sources and sets up his notes for the minilesson.

Give one additional tip, which is that when checking fake news, it helps to actively seek sources that tend to represent different viewpoints or constituents.

"Researchers, we found a lot of discrepancies, didn't we? It appears that these kids weren't arrested for free speech; they were arrested for trespassing. They weren't just handing out copies of the Constitution, like the video claimed. They were soliciting for a national college youth group. So fascinating. Maybe the video shouldn't be called 'When Free Speech Gets You Arrested.' It should be called, 'When Trespassing Gets You Arrested.'

"I want to give you one last tip. Whenever you are checking fake news, to avoid confirmation bias, you want to seek sources that are measured, careful, and thorough in presenting evidence."

LINK

Stir kids up to be better than the many of us adults who passively accept fake news (or even create it). Alert them to the upcoming debates, and send them off to review their research.

"Researchers, this is advanced critical thinking. A lot of adults accept fake news without questioning it, all the time. They read tabloids, they watch so-called news channels that distort events, and mostly, they don't try to check by going to multiple sources. I think of myself as being highly educated, and I didn't even ask about the possibility of fake news. I'm too accepting of media.

"But you can be different. You can be better. You can intelligently seek out varied sources all the time. You can get used to reading or watching the news from channels or papers that tend to disagree. Not just for the debates you'll engage in, or the talks you'll give, but for the world you'll live in and affect, the world needs you to be intelligent, fair, and ethical.

"Tomorrow you'll be engaging in flash-debates. That means you'll argue your position, and you may argue the opposite position, to test out strengths and weaknesses of your stance. Take today to look back over your research and fill in any holes. And as you do so, add in this strategy, which is to remain alert to the possibility of fake news, and do some fact-checking as needed."

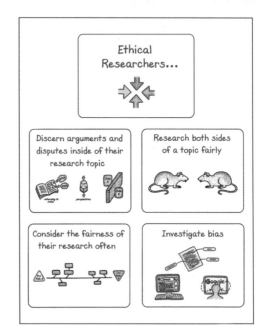

Planning Independent Work with Debates and Presentations in Mind

Y OU'VE BEEN REMINDING STUDENTS that they'll be giving impassioned flash-debates at the end of this bend, and that they'll follow those debates up with more formal TED talks. Now is a good time to check that kids have these deadlines in mind, and are using the skills they learned in the first part of the unit, as well as those they are learning now. For instance, have they been taking lean notes? Have they been synthesizing those notes? Are they thinking about how to include group members, and harness their strengths?

You might gather students in their study groups, and offer support as needed. Here are some likely scenarios.

Supporting Students with Independent Work with a Presentation Approaching	
If . . .	**Then . . .**
Students seem to have few notes to work from . . .	Suggest that rather than doing new research, they return to the texts they've read and watched, and jot lean notes on the main points as well as specific evidence that they can use in their arguments.
Students have an overwhelming amount of notes to work from . . .	Remind them to take the time to synthesize. Suggest that they might create an infographic to use in their flash-debate. Remind them that they can create these infographics by hand or using a software program.
Study groups are dominated by one or two students . . .	Revisit your coaching along the introvert-extrovert continuum. Invite students to reflect on how they are using the strategies you've offered. Especially gather your extroverts and coach them in bringing in other voices and facilitating discussions.
Students' positions remain simplistic, binary, or lacking multiple perspectives . . .	Suggest they revisit their position, this time taking the alternate viewpoint and really trying to explain a few valid points inside that viewpoint. Have them then practice reasoned language to acknowledge multiple ideas.
Students' positions seem well supported . . .	Suggest they work on presentation skills, by rehearsing and getting feedback from others.

Checking Work Plans with Deadlines in Mind

Remind students of tomorrow's flash-debates and let them know precisely when they will be giving their TED talks, as well as the parameters of those talks. Set them up to make work plans with their study groups.

"You have time to check in with your group. Whenever you have a deadline approaching, you want to make sure that you've thought through your work plans with that deadline in mind.

"For instance, you know that tomorrow you'll flash-debate. Then on this date (I pointed to the calendar), you'll give more formal TED talks. You might make a calendar of the number of days until you give your TED talks. For your debates, you mostly want to harness your evidence. Then for your talks, you'll want to begin to think about visuals, and what you want to show as well as what you want to say. Talk to your group. What work plans do you need to make? Set your own homework, for each of you."

SESSION 16 HOMEWORK

 PREPARING TO FLASH-DEBATE

Today you set work plans with your study group. Knowing that your flash-debate is tomorrow, think about how you want to organize your argument, what evidence you may want to include, and what notes you'll use. Tonight, work toward those goals.

Flash-Debating to Rehearse Preliminary Arguments (and See Counterclaims)

Dear Teachers,

Today, we suggest that you organize students to flash-debate both sides of their arguments. Even though many of them may have now moved toward supporting one position or side, these flash-debates will help them consider and give voice to counterclaims. Some students in each group, then, will need to briefly argue positions that might oppose their own. Suggest that kids who are good at arguing try this more onerous task—and that they'll come away with more thinking about how to address counterclaims.

There are a few goals here. One is that kids who learn to debate learn to "speak in essays." They learn to build logical structure, they learn to work with text evidence, and all of this talk is great rehearsal for writing or other kinds of publishing such as their upcoming TED talks. Another goal is for students to begin to hear the strengths and weaknesses of their positions—which parts have very strong evidence, which reasoning is fully developed, and which parts are weaker. Yet another goal is for students to more fully consider counterclaims. Both by listening to their opponent and by switching sides, they'll learn more about other perspectives inside the argument they are researching.

You'll do a variety of coaching. Most of this will be around logical reasoning, structure, and unpacking evidence. Some of your coaching will be on presentation skills. Set aside any attempt to fit this all into the classic minilesson structure! Today will be grand guided practice. It's really engaging; kids work intensely, and you get to give a lot of targeted, lean feedback. We've provided some possible feedback tips in the online resources—mainly, coaching students to articulate a big bold claim, to consider sequence and transitions, ways to frame evidence, and word choice. 👆

You'll probably want to collect notebooks at the end of this bend, again. If you use the checklist/rubric that we've provided, you'll be assessing items 4, 5, and 6 in this bend. Give students a chance to self-assess as well, so that you can see how closely their self-assessment aligns with yours. This tool is in the online resources for this session. 👆

119

Have in mind (and remind kids), that they'll publish at the end of Bend III with TED talks, and so these flash-debates are a rehearsal for the positions they'll present in those talks. Today they'll find out a lot about the strengths and weaknesses of their positions.

If you've paired students (within study groups of four) then you might suggest that students each caucus, or rehearse, one side of the argument with a partner, and then they each debate one-on-one against an opponent in their group or partnerships could debate another partnership. In any case, make sure kids tell their opponents what their best points were—what they were struck by.

The biggest goal here is for kids to become aware of a paradigm in which they are arguing to learn, not arguing to win. This country, and the world, needs more citizens who can listen as well as persuade.

All the best,
Mary and Marc

Flash-Debating to Rehearse Arguments	
Argument Moves	**Predictable Coaching**
1. In their study groups, kids name two opposing positions in their arguments, so that each partnership will argue one side against another partnership within their study group. Students may decide to argue one-on-one against each other while partners take notes, offer support, and so on.	• Support kids in coming up with clear claims. Clarify that they represent opposed positions and that they have big, bold claims. Visit with study groups, saying things like, "It seems like you're saying . . ." and "Let's review your positions. Maybe one way to say your claim could be . . ."
2. Partnerships organize their arguments using their notes and texts as sources, and their notebooks as a place to jot presentation notes—probably boxes and bullets.	• Coach kids in organizing their arguments into parts, often sorting evidence under reasons or ways. For example, "One way teen expression should be protected is by educating principals . . ." • Some kids may need support with which evidence goes with which point. For kids who need a lot of support, help them make cards with text evidence that they can sort and use as notes. • Invite students to rank their evidence and reasons and to consider sequence. ("Do you want to start with your strongest, or end with it?")

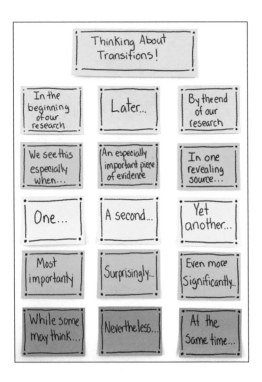

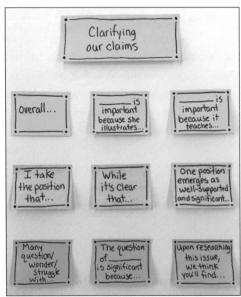

Argument Moves	Predictable Coaching
3. Partnerships rehearse their arguments, figuring out who will say what, and how they'll begin, including stating an introduction.	• Coach students to provide context for the argument in the introduction. • Coach students to forecast their argument in the introduction. • Remind students of presentation strategies: body language, gestures, tone of voice, eye contact.
4. Partnerships debate—usually they have between one and three minutes each to make their argument.	• As they debate, coach debaters to use their notes. • Coach opponents to jot notes. • Coach students to consider counterclaims. • Remind debaters of body language, gestures, tone of voice, eye contact.
5. Opponents tell each other what their best points were—what were they convinced by? They can also compliment each other on any specific presentation skills.	• Coach students to jot these points, so they can acknowledge and/or rebut counterarguments.
6. Study groups "regroup" to consider strengths and holes in their arguments and to make plans for next steps in research and strengthening their positions in preparation for upcoming TED talks.	• Remind students to jot notes on what they are thinking, while it's fresh in their minds. • Suggest they revisit their text sets, deciding what to read next, and if they need to seek more sources. • Give feedback on how to quote sources by saying something about the source, as well as leading into and out of evidence. • Offer a variety of possible tips and invite students to reflect on ways to strengthen their arguments and debates.

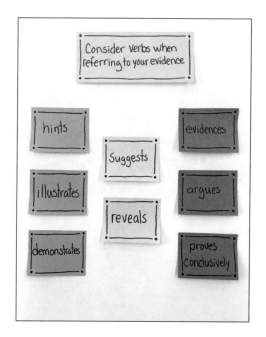

Notebook Checklist			
Research Notebooks	Somewhat	Consistently	Yes!
1. I've kept track of sources, developing a system that let's me return to texts and reference them accurately			
2. I've developed a system for collecting significant vocabulary terms and concepts			
3. I've gone back into my notes, annotating, re-organizing, synthesizing			
4. As my research progressed, I've taken deeper, more detailed notes, varying my note-taking structures to match my purpose			
5. My notes show evidence of how my thinking has developed and changed over time - writing to think, reflection, analysis			
6. My research notes show the fairness of my research - I have researched multiple perspectives			

A Letter to Teachers

Dear Colleagues,

This is a short bend, with only four sessions. In these sessions, you'll set your students to study TED talks, especially TED talks given by young people. Your students will study the purpose of TED talks, which is almost always to both teach and persuade. They'll study the craft of public speaking and presenting. And then they'll give it a try. Your students won't need written scripts for these talks, but they will need presentation notes, visuals, and a plan. They'll also need time to rehearse, as well as some tips on ways to raise the level of their talks. We've tried to provide that teaching in these sessions.

The content of kids' talks will come from their research. Your students have spent a few weeks researching—first building background knowledge and then investigating disputes inside their topic. They've learned to work as study partners, to take charge of their own reading and research, to tailor their notes to match their purposes, and to use their notebooks to synthesize information. Most recently, they've taken up critical research practices, learning to confront their own biases and those of the texts they read, to understand how search engines confirm their predispositions and stances, and to be alert to the possibility of fake news.

Frankly, by now, your students have learned more critical research practices than many of us have as adults. All of these research skills will help your students to be more informed, critical citizens. These skills will help kids in content classes in high school and college. These skills will build students' confidence in their academic identities.

We haven't spoken enough, though, of how kids not only become more skilled, they also become more knowledgeable and impassioned about their topic. Now you'll harness that passion to help your students become more vocal and articulate and activist. Collaborative talks give students ways to merge their strengths and build new strengths. They are engaging, achievable, and significant.

You can decide how to publish these talks that students give. For the ambitious, you might set your class to publishing on YouTube. For the slightly more cautious, you might publish on your school website, or on a class website, or Google classroom. We've been amazed how seriously kids take these talks, even when they are publishing inside of class. It does help to be clear about the intended age level of their audience, since one of the easiest ways to raise the level of argumentation is to tailor your argument to your audience. We suggest, therefore, that even if adults may view these talks, kids think mostly about shifting the thinking of other kids. Future voters and informed citizens all, your students will learn to engage in civic action even now.

Don't fret about whether or not your kids' talks end up with precisely clear structure, impeccable referencing, lots of academic language, or interesting camera angles. We've included some samples in the online resources and you'll see they are impassioned and rough cut. You're doing a beautiful job if your kids have learned to care—if they want to reach others with what they've learned, and if they're willing to take risks to accomplish their goals.

All the best,
Mary and Marc

Read-Aloud

Starting with Mentors: Teen TED Talks

IN THIS SESSION

TODAY you'll lead students in a guided inquiry and analysis of TED talks to examine both the structure and craft of the genre.

TODAY YOUR STUDENTS will analyze two TED talks given by teens, noticing how the structure is different than a typical essay-type structure. They'll work with their study group to make a plan for their own TED talk.

GETTING READY

✔ Be prepared to watch the beginning of the TED talk "Our Campaign to Ban Plastic Bags in Bali," presented by Melati and Isabel Wijsen, as well as "Hackschooling Makes Me Happy," presented by Logan LaPlante. A link to the TED talk is available in the online resources (see Conducting the Read-Aloud). ✄

✔ Have students sit with a partner from a different study group in the meeting area (see Connection).

✔ Students should have their notebooks at the meeting area for the inquiry, and they'll also need Post-it notes.

✔ Start a new anchor chart for the bend, "Activist Researchers . . ." (see Link). ✄

CONNECTION

Inspire kids to try a one-minute rally speech, saying something about the significance of their argument, and luring others to their position.

"Researchers, I want you to try something. Without opening your notebook, without looking back over your texts, I want you to think about why the argument you've been researching is important. Why should others care about this topic? Like, I'm thinking about fourteen-year-old climate warrior Xiuhtezcatl, and how he spoke so passionately about what he saw as big companies destroying natural resources in his community. And his position is that speaking up, banding together, can change those practices.

"Think for a moment about your own topic and your position, and when you have some thoughts about why it all matters, put a thumb up, or give a nod.

"Quickly, decide which of you will be Partner 1 and who will be Partner 2, and make sure you'll be talking to someone from a different study group." I gave them a moment to set up. "Okay, you're going to try giving one-minute rally speeches. Partner 1, you're first. Five-four-three-two-one—make us care in one minute!"

Listen in as the first partners give their rally speeches, and be prepared to compliment their passion and/or their knowledge. Then coach Partner 2s about the importance of using body language and their tone of voice.

"Nice work, Partner 1s! It was especially impressive how much you all know about your topic, that you could talk like that without notes! A lot of you made a clear plea for change, or stated a claim you have for what's right. Partner 2, here's a tip before you go. Use your body as well as your mind to make us care. Think about gestures, and a passionate tone of voice! Five-four-three-two-one, go Partner 2s!"

After Partner 2s give their speeches, gather students' attention back and introduce the move from research to presenting, specifically through TED talks.

"Researchers, you know a lot about your topics, the debates inside those topics, and your positions now. That means that you're ready to become activists, to teach and sway others. One way to reach people with your ideas is through social media, and one of the most powerful forms of that is the TED talk, a form of social media developed expressly to bring an audience's attention to ideas they may not have thought a lot about.

"It always makes sense to get to know a genre before you try it out yourself. So let's watch parts of a couple of TED talks given by kids your age, and think about what we notice these kids doing, and how we can give effective talks like these."

Introduce an inquiry question.

"It seems like the most important inquiry question for you to investigate today will be: How do TED talks go?" I jotted:

How do TED talks go?

CONDUCTING THE READ-ALOUD

Set students up to first watch the beginning of a TED talk through an inquiry lens. Invite students to have their notebooks open so they can jot about any parts as they watch.

"To figure that out, it seems like you want to think a bit about the overall purpose of the presentation—what the author or speaker is trying to do. And since you will be planning your own presentation, it seems like it would also be helpful to figure out some of the parts of a successful TED talk." I added these questions.

How do TED talks go?

- What is the speaker hoping to accomplish?
- What are the different parts of the talk?

"Let's watch the beginning of this talk, which is called, 'Our Campaign to Ban Plastic Bags in Bali.' It's presented by two sisters from Bali, named Melati and Isabel." I jotted those names and the title on a big Post-it. As you watch, will you have your notebook open? I think you'll figure out the purpose of the talk very quickly, but also be ready to capture notes about some of the parts.

"In fact, either take a few Post-its and stick them into your notebook, or sketch four or five boxes, and that way, each time you think the talk moves to a new part, you can jot down what kind of part it is, and you'll have a kind of storyboard for the talk. Like you might write on a Post-it 'Funny story to introduce the topic' or you might write 'a list of solutions' or you might write 'What other people say about topic' or 'Scientific evidence.'"

Play the beginning of Melati and Isabel's talk, and quietly do some jotting as well, capturing some of the parts as an informal storyboard.

"Ready? Your notebook is set up? Let's watch the first couple of minutes or so. As you watch, think about your inquiry questions. What's the purpose of this talk? And how does it go?"

I played the first two minutes of the TED talk, then invited students to compare their thinking with a partner.

Listen to how kids describe the overall purpose of this TED talk and some of the parts, and then summarize some of what they say, giving a tip about paying attention to emotional content.

"It seems like you're all saying that overall, the first part of this talk is sort of an introduction to the problem. The girls don't even introduce themselves, but instead they go right into how plastic is destroying their paradise. 'Explain a problem.' So that's one part, and in this TED Talk, they explain the problem right at the beginning.

"Now let's think about the purpose. A lot of you said that it seems like so far, the purpose of Melati and Isabel's TED talk is to teach their audience about how they got plastic bags banned in Bali. You might change your thinking on that later, when you've watched more. For now, let me give you one tip—think about how presenters stir your emotions. Would it be fair to say that these girls also want us to *care about* how Bali is getting polluted with plastic bags?

"So . . . so far, Melati and Isabel want us to care about Bali getting polluted, and they want to teach about their campaign to ban plastic bags. And they *start* by introducing the way the island is in danger of becoming an island of trash."

TED Talk Mentors		
Presenters	Structure	Style
Aaron Huey "America's Native Prisoners of War"	Pictures Introduction Provides Background Metaphor Evidence with Elaboration Map	Pictures TimeLine Pauses Powerful Vocabulary Creates Empathy by modeling emotions Eye Contact
Logan Laplante "Hack Schooling" Argument Style	Strong Introduction Clear Claim Made Connections Evidence Posed Questions Clear Conclusion	Hand Gestures Moved Right and Left Eye Contact Used Humor Named the audiences "Inner Thinking" Pauses Visual Supports Poetic Language
Melati and Isabel Wijsen "Plastic Bag Informational Style	Strong Introduction to Hook audience Clear Roles Presented a problem Asked Audience Questions Ideas supported with evidence Powerful Conclusion Made Connections Used Quotes	Inspirational Hand Gestures Smiled Eye Contact Varied Volume Interacted with each other Conversational Inspired and Challenged audience to make change

FIG. 18–1   Marc charted the class discussion as they analyzed the beginnings of some mentor TED talks.

Set kids up to listen and watch again, this time with new inquiry lenses, ones that will help them analyze how this talk works—the parts of it. Then summarize and share using either a student's storyboard or your own.

"It's interesting, because Melati and Isabel don't come right out and say, 'No one in Bali should use plastic bags.' That's not how they begin their talk—they don't say what they want people to do, they don't make their main argument right away. So, clearly, TED talks are not structured exactly like argument essays or position papers with claims, reasons, evidence, and attention to counterclaims. Let's figure out how these presenters do make their points then. See if you can fill in some of your boxes with the parts of their talk. We'll watch a few more minutes of the talk this time."

I started the TED talk at the beginning again, and this time we watched until 5:35.

"Jot down some parts that you noticed, then go ahead, compare with your partner. What are you noticing?"

Ban Plastic Bags in Bali

Introduces the problem right away, supporting with visuals	Introduces their relationship to the issue–almost as a story	Shares a list of lessons

Sum up some of what students have noticed, especially that TED talks approach an argument less formally (and more artistically) than some other kinds of arguments, speeches, and presentations.

"We're definitely noticing that a TED talk doesn't just come out with a claim, reasons, and evidence, 'You should stop using plastic bags! Here are three reasons! Here is our evidence!' Instead, a TED talk lures you in. It gives you context, it gets you to understand and care about the problem, it tells you a bit of a story. Here, Isabel and Melati start with an introduction, to the problem and to the speakers. Then they begin to tell a story, and a lot of us noticed that the girls set their story up as a problem—the bags—and their solution—their campaign."

Introduce a second TED talk, "Hackschooling Makes Me Happy," inviting students to do similar thinking as they study this second mentor text.

"Let's take a look at another talk, since probably not all talks go the exact same way. This one is presented by a boy, Logan LaPlante. Logan's an incredible athlete. He's one of the best young competitive freestyle skiers, and he lives out in Lake Tahoe. Logan's talk about what schools should be teaching went viral. In fact, if you

Teachers, as you listen to kids and document what they say, you can also elevate it, by saying it back with just a little more academic language, or a little more clarity. Often kids are on the edge of some big thinking, and they are reaching for the language for it. A little coauthoring helps them find those words.

Teachers, you'll know your kids, and the kinds of talks they'll enjoy, and what might get in the way of them being open to presentations. Giving a little context, a kind of text introduction, can help orient kids to the presenter.

go to his website, he talks about how, if he'd known his video would go viral, maybe he would have cut his hair or not worn a pink hat. But I love when kids are unafraid to be themselves."

I motioned to their notebooks. "Jot some new boxes, or take some more Post-its. This talk is called 'Hackschooling Makes Me Happy.' Let's see if you can figure out first, what's the overall purpose of his presentation, and then also, what are some of the parts."

I played the first few minutes, until 5:20.

After kids watch, jot, and talk, summarize again, once again showing an example of a storyboard.

Hackschooling

Poses a question	Shares some research	Introduces the problem and his big idea	Explains a list of solutions

"So interesting. This TED talk wants to do the same thing—get you to think about a new idea. But Logan does it differently than Melati and Isabel. Where they mostly tell a story, his talk is much more idea based. He shares research, and quotes others. He does talk about himself, but the parts of his talk are more academic."

LINK

Send students off with their study group, to begin to outline possible parts of their TED talk, and to think about the work they want to accomplish.

"What matters here, researchers, is that these teens, like Xiuhtezcatl, care deeply about their ideas, and they want others to care. You have ideas, too. I bet you have some thoughts now about how to convey those ideas. Will you tell stories? Will you share visuals and images? Will you share research? Will you start with your idea, like Melati and Isabel did, or bring your audience on more of a journey, as Logan did?

"It seems like the best use of your time now would be for your study group to get together and begin to outline some of the parts of your talk. Will you begin with your claim, or end with it? Will you provide context at the beginning, or start with a gripping story? Remember, your talk doesn't have to be just like Melati and Isabel's or Logan's. It needs to be yours. Off you go to work with your study group. I'll start a new anchor chart, to help you with your TED-like talks."

Kids get used to having their notebooks out regularly in the meeting area.

ANCHOR CHART

Activist Researchers . . .

• **Choose a way to stir emotions in others**
• **Study mentor texts to get ideas for speaking and presenting**

Choose a way to stir emotions in others

Study mentor texts to get ideas for speaking and presenting

INDEPENDENT WORK

Charting Some Planning Structures for Talks

Without a doubt, most of your kids will need to spend all of their time beginning to envision how their talk might go. Some of the study groups may work together. In other study groups, kids may have broken into partnerships. So these talks will be given by two to four students. Our best advice to you is to help groups capture their ideas. Someone in the group needs to begin to storyboard, or outline, or start a flowchart. You might consider sharing a few sample graphics as examples.

For students who may struggle with these looser, more hybrid structures, you can suggest a simple structure of context/problem/plea for change.

Other students, though, will be willing to think about how *part* of their talk will be a structured argument, but other parts may be more aimed at the emotions than the intellect—anecdotes, narratives, profiles, case studies, and so on. This is a good time for your kids to be brave with structure. Tomorrow, kids will work entirely on structure. If they make a start at thinking about that today, they'll be better positioned to really work out their parts tomorrow. And they may revise again after that.

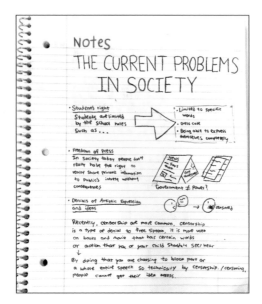

FIG. 18–2   Tao plans the start of a TED talk in his notebook.

SHARE

Set kids up to rehearse a part of their talk with someone tonight. Encourage them to notice how it goes. Make sure partners have taken care of each other in terms of rehearsal buddies.

"Activists, tomorrow you'll work with your group to get your talk planned, and to begin to fill in the parts; who might say what, and what you'll show as well as say. Today you made a start at planning. Remember, these won't be essays, they'll be talks. And the best way to work on talks is . . . to talk. So tonight, try out part of your talk on somebody. It could be a friend, or a family member, or a teacher. Notice how much you can say in under three minutes. Get some feedback on parts that work. Notice your pacing and your tone of voice.

"Right now, talk to your partner. Who can you practice part of your talk on? Make sure your partner has a rehearsal buddy, too. Volunteer if needed. Make a plan for what part you want to rehearse—what you want to talk about, and who you want to try it on."

SESSION 18 HOMEWORK

STUDYING YOURSELF AS YOU REHEARSE

Tonight, practice part of your talk on somebody who can give you feedback. Notice what goes well and what doesn't. Pay attention to your content, and also to your body language and eye contact. Learn from this rehearsal!

FIG. 18–3   Kids film part of their talks as a rehearsal to prepare and give each other feedback.

Authoring Work Plans and Putting Them into Action

IN THIS SESSION

TODAY you'll teach students that as they move from collaborative research to presentation, it's important to develop a work plan, put it into action, and then use that plan as a checklist to move through the process.

TODAY YOUR STUDENTS will devise a list of tasks that need to be accomplished to prepare for their upcoming talks. The collaborative work plan will become a checklist that students will use to guide their preparation. Study groups will meet today.

MINILESSON

CONNECTION

Let students know that you are aware of the anxiety that come from oral presentations, but that a collaborative work plan can help alleviate stress and focus energy in positive ways.

"Okay, soon-to-be TED talkers, I've talked with a lot of you about your TED-style talks, and what I'm getting from you is . . . nervousness. You're nervous about your speaking and presentation skills, you're nervous about how to organize your talk, and mostly, you're nervous about getting it done.

"Pretty much every writer, and everyone who is getting ready to make a presentation, finds that starting it is the hardest part. Once you get something—anything—started, then you start feeling better.

"So today, you need work time. But I thought I might help you with how to get the most out of this work time, because it's both more fun and trickier to figure out a workflow when you are working collaboratively."

♣ **Name the teaching point.**

"I want to remind you that when you are moving from research to presentation, especially when you are working with a group, it's going to be crucial to develop a work plan and to put that plan into action. A powerful work plan acts as a checklist—it lays out what needs to get done, so you can work together to meet deadlines."

TEACHING AND ACTIVE ENGAGEMENT

Share examples of professionals who use checklists. Then, engage students in the work of creating a master work plan in the form of a collaborative checklist.

"So, listen, if we were pilots, and we were getting ready to fly a passenger plane, we would have a checklist."

I showed some flight checklists used by airline pilots that I pulled up on Google Images.

"Pilots and flight crews have checklists because there are so many things they need to make sure are taken care of, and they don't want to forget anything. They especially don't want to forget something under the stress of flight.

"Presenting can also be stressful, and when we're stressed, we can get overwhelmed and then we tend to forget stuff. So it can be really helpful to create a work plan that is essentially a checklist, whenever you are involved in a project. It turns out that there is research that shows that just making a list helps you get some control over what you need to do. It calms you down, and focuses you.

"Whenever you need to create your own checklist, it's helpful to jot a bunch of things that you think will be important to do. If you were writing an essay, you might think about the parts of the essay, or about your process. For something like this, where you are pulling together research, making some visuals, rehearsing, you probably want to think about both what goes *in* a TED talk—what did you see when you watched Isabel, Melati, and Logan?—and what's involved in *preparing* for a talk like this."

Ask students to individually think about tasks for preparing for a TED talk, and have them jot their ideas on Post-its. Then have them share with their study group, to create a master checklist.

"Let's try that now. Here are some Post-its. Without talking to your study group yet, try jotting down some of the tasks you imagine your group needs to accomplish to get your talk ready. Jot only one task on each Post-it, so you can put them in order. One tip. Use the pronoun *we*. When we say "We need to" or "I need to," it helps us take responsibility."

I gave students a moment to do that work, listening in, giving advice, and looking for examples to share.

Teachers, the best book on this is Atul Gawande's fabulous The Checklist Manifesto. *The* Guardian *also has an article called, "The Psychology of the To-Do List—Why Your Brain Loves Ordered Tasks." In full disclosure, the counterclaim is that sometimes making lists gives the illusion of progress, or a long list can overwhelm the creator. If your students have been in our writing units, they'll be used to using checklists to self-assess their progress. Here, you help them create their own checklist.*

"Now, share your Post-it notes with your group, and work to create a master work plan. What task might come first? What next?"

Share some examples, which may include ones from different groups, and one you've provided. Invite groups to add to their own checklists.

"Let's take a look at some examples. Will you look at these, and will you add any tasks to your checklist, that feel important?"

I showed some samples and invited study groups to add tasks to their own checklists.

Give a tip, namely that sometimes as presenters rehearse, they realize it will be helpful to return to their research texts and/or notes.

"These are some great work plans! I do have one tip. That is, that as you prepare and rehearse, you may find that you need to return to your research—either to the texts or to your notes—to fill in parts of your talk. Let's add that to your work plan, so you remember.

"And one more thing—remember to support each other. Remember all we did to think about harnessing our different strengths and to bring out our strengths in a group. Think about your group, and each person inside of it, and make this beautiful for everyone."

I added:

> • Return to research texts and notes as needed to strengthen our talk.
> • Support each other with each part of the work.

LINK

Send study groups off to work on the tasks on their work plan. Remind them to use tools such as infographics and synthesis pages that may be useful in their presentations.

"Let's send you off to work, but before we do, let's think about what that work will look like. It seems like you'll take a minute or two to divvy up these tasks. Perhaps all of you should begin to lay out the parts of your talk, and then once you've figured out the parts, some might fill in some of the research, while others create visuals—and remember that you've got infographics and synthesis pages you can show.

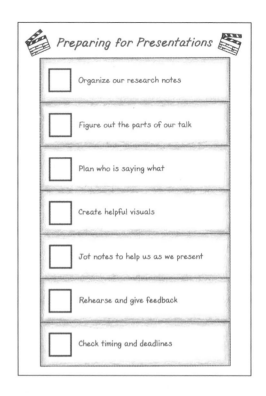

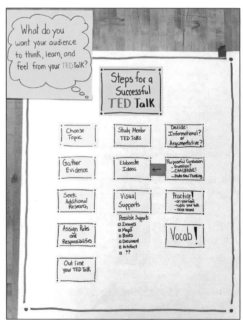

"You have today to get your talk mostly ready. Your talk will be three minutes long. You want a good draft of it finished today, so tomorrow you can work on raising the level."

I added to our anchor chart.

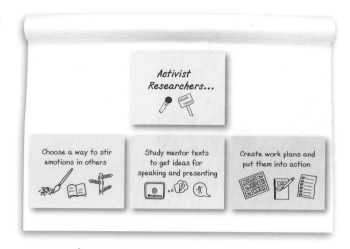

ANCHOR CHART

Activist Researchers . . .

- Choose a way to stir emotions in others
- Study mentor texts to get ideas for speaking and presenting
- **Create work plans and put them into action**

Grappling with Structure: Supporting a Progression of Structural Choices

YOUR STUDENTS ARE MOVING toward giving their TED-style talks, which tend to be less formal, more artful presentations of arguments. In her TED talk on the power of introverts, for example, Susan Cain argues that introvertism can be a strength, and she presents a variety of anecdotes and research points to support that claim. In his TED talk on motivation, Daniel Pink argues that external rewards are, in fact, ineffective in creating lasting, deeply felt motivation, and then he shares research and stories to make his point. TED talks vary in how they are put together. Yet all of them have some kind of underlying organizational structure.

For many of you teachers, and a lot of students, this looser structure will feel very freeing, and you'll run with it. You and the kids can think about simply the parts of these talks, and you'll feel comfortable with a more artful, playful structure. But it may be that you are linking this unit with students writing position papers, or you are interested in supporting some students with traditional argument essay structure. If so, here are ways to support a progression of structural choices.

Supporting Structure in Argument, from Simple to Playful	
If . . .	**Then . . .**
Students find it easiest to structure their argument as **claim and examples** . . .	Help students lay out their evidence and consider the order they want to present it in, with a simple boxes-and-bullets format. Have them rehearse by putting a Post-it at each bullet, with the evidence they'll use as an example, and saying their argument aloud. You can also help students think about transitions. They might use simple transitions such as: *for example*, *also*, *in addition*, *finally*. Or they might use transitions that reflect some deliberate sequencing, such as: *most significantly*, *surprisingly*, *even more importantly*.
Students are ready to organize their argument with **ways/kinds/reasons** . . .	Suggest that students try these different kinds of subcategories. • For example, suggest students might try out ways. "There are a few ways that students get in trouble for expressing themselves. One way is through what they wear. Another way is through what they say." • Then suggest they might try kinds. "The cases that have come up in the Supreme Court that test free speech tend to be of two kinds. One kind is where administrators have . . . Another kind is where other students . . ." • They might also try reasons. "One reason students tend to test free speech rights is that the original first amendment wasn't clear about the age at which constitutional rights are protected. Another reason is that sometimes the First Amendment of free speech might interfere with the Fourteenth Amendment right to an education . . ."

If . . .	Then . . .
Students are ready to work with **counterclaims** in their arguments . . .	Suggest that students consider where they will address the counterclaim, and try rehearsing different ways. Two common structures include: • Launching with the counterclaim, then shifting to claim. "Some argue that . . . and this stance has some validity . . . for example . . . Let's look at the other side now, though, as it turns out . . ." • Addressing counterclaim in each point. "While some say . . . nevertheless . . ." It may be useful to provide students with cards for each part of their essay, and/or more sophisticated transitional phrases. We provide these as a resource in the online resources.
Students are ready for more **fluid, artful structures** . . .	We suggest that you look at Katherine Bomer's fabulous book, *The Journey Is Everything*, about journey of thought essays, and/or Tom Romano's fabulous book, *Crafting Authentic Voice*, about valuing voice over formulaic structure. Both these texts are favorites of ours, and we firmly believe that lots, and maybe all, students are ready to play with structure. You and they need to be okay with their attempts not always working out all that well at first. Often, even if structure gets obscured, voice and quirky reasoning become stronger. It can be helpful to think about parts, then, that don't have to occur in any specific order, such as: • Leads, lures, and hooks • Context and theories or inquiry questions • Anecdotes (may include humor or other emotional appeals) • Research evidence and quoting authorities • Being fair to other sides • Closure and claims It might be helpful for students to lay out the parts of their talk on index cards.

Matching Presenters to Parts—the Give and Take of Collaborative Talks

Guide students to work in their study group and make a plan for how they will share the actual oral presentation of their talk.

"Presenters, you've got a plan for your talk. You've thought through the parts, and what you might say in each part—your reasoning, your evidence, and so on. Now you need to figure out who is speaking when. You'll remember that Melati and Isabel went back and forth in their TED talk seamlessly, so that both of them spoke often, and sometimes even shared parts.

"Take some time now to review the parts of your talk, and match presenters to each part. Who will start, and give some kind of introduction or lead into your talk? What parts might you share?"

SESSION 19 HOMEWORK

 ### ELICITING FEEDBACK ON YOUR PRESENTATION SKILLS

Tonight, practice the part of your talk that has been given to you as a presenter. Choose someone who can give you feedback. Notice what goes well and what doesn't. Pay attention to your content, and also to your body language and eye contact. Try it again if your audience is willing.

Raising the Level of Talks

Dear Teachers,

Today we suggest that students collaborate with their study groups to not only work on their three-minute talks, but also raise the level of these talks. Rather than gathering everyone for a minilesson, we suggest that students move through three different centers, all of which are available in the online resources. You'll briefly introduce these centers, and suggest that students might spend about ten minutes per center, and then meet with their group to get to work, applying some of what they learned in the center to their own preparation. Study groups might decide that all of them will visit one center together, or that they will divide up, and visit more than one center, reporting back to their group with some important skills they want to try.

Of course, you may decide to stretch this session over two days, to give students more time to visit centers, to prepare and to rehearse. We promise you, though, that we have seen kids pull together short TED talks in a short time. They are only going to have three minutes to present, and so they'll want to focus on their most important research and provocative thinking. Think of how daily live TV shows have to pull together material every single day!

Here are brief descriptions of the centers we've found particularly helpful, which you can print from the online resources. The first reviews the structural work you started in the launch of this bend. If you have a study group who is still struggling to organize their talk, you may want to join the group at this center. Have extra copies of centers so students can go to their favorites.

Center 1: How Do Great TED Talks Tend to Go? Thinking More Deeply about What to Include

TED talks are more informal and more anecdotal than formal speeches or debates. Their goal is to interest their audience as well as to inform. For this center, you'll choose a short TED talk. You will also have a set of cards, which describe various parts of TED talks. As you watch the Ted talk, you'll try to put these cards in order, to capture the internal structure of the talk. Then you'll want to decide on which of these parts will be helpful in your talk, and what order you might put them in. One hint—boxes and bullets may be only one part of a Ted talk.

Everyday Leadership, by Drew Dudley
Hackschooling Makes Me Happy, by Logan LaPlante

Center 2: What Interesting Craft Techniques Can We Steal from Artful Ted Talks?

Great Ted talks get their audiences interested in their topic in lots of creative ways. The speakers lure their audience to care, and they lure their audience to their viewpoint, both with research and by how they introduce their arguments. Here, you'll choose a TED talk and watch the beginning of it. You also have a set of Techniques and Goals Charts. As you watch the TED talk, you'll look for examples of these techniques. Pause the video when you find one, to think about what makes that technique compelling, and what goal the author achieved. At the end, you'll want to consider some of your goals, and which techniques you may want to try in your own talk.

The Puzzle of Motivation, by Dan Pink
America's Native Prisoners of War, by Aaron Huey

Center 3: Incredible Speakers Teach Us about Public Speaking

Great speakers not only say important words. They use their voice, their body, their expressions, their emotions, to mesmerize their audience. Here, you'll choose among speakers who have moved millions, and you'll study them as they give a speech. You'll consider a few moves these speakers make, that you can try when you are publicly speaking in your TED talk (and in other times when your words matter).

Cory Booker Williams Commencement Speech 2011
Emma Gonzalez's "March for Our Lives" speech
Naomi Wadler's "March for Our Lives" speech
"How to Speak So that People Want to Listen"—TED Talk by Julian Treasure

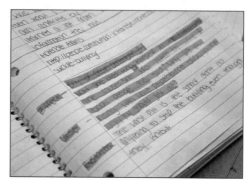

FIG. 20–1   Kids return to their resources— their shared tools, text sets, and notebooks— to prepare their TED talks.

After students have had a chance to learn from some of these centers, set them to work preparing and rehearsing. Clearly, kids should try run-throughs, which will highlight for them which parts are going well, which parts need clearer reasoning, or a helpful visual, or attention to louder voices, or slower pacing.

You could add to the anchor chart.

> **ANCHOR CHART**
>
> Activist Researchers . . .
>
> • Choose a way to stir emotions in others
> • Study mentor texts to get ideas for speaking and presenting
> • Create work plans and put them into action
> • **Organize their talks with an underlying structure**
> • **Use craft techniques to engage their audience**
> • **Work with their voice, gestures, expressions, and emotions**

You can act as a proficient partner, an attentive and helpfully critical audience, or a coach, as study groups work. Remind kids to use their vocabulary cards. Remind them to consider their audience. Help them consider why this topic matters, and what they want their audience to know, think, and feel. Compliment their strengths, and coach into problem areas.

It will be a little crazy, and a lot of fun.

All the best,
Mary and Marc

Celebrating Content and Reflecting on Opportunities for Transfer

Dear Teachers,

Today your students will give their TED-style talks. You may decide to film them, in which case it can be helpful to have a site in the room where you've set up a backdrop, and you've set kids up with a device to film. You can then upload these videos to a shared site such as a Padlet or Google Drive or a closed YouTube channel. You'll see some photos and videos of kids filming in our online resources. If you can set up two sites in your classroom, more kids can film.

We've found it helpful to have a chart that lists the order of TED talk presentations. If you are using two sites for TED talk presentations this chart will be helpful for you to establish a balance of topics and presentation levels. The chart also makes public for the students the structure and order for the TED talk event. Any unexpected changes can be negotiated with the students and reflected on the chart.

Keep in mind that a well-defined TED talk site will be helpful to establish the boundary between the stage for the presenters, the area for the students as audience, and the area for student(s) who are filming to have an unobstructed view of the presentations. Having a well-defined TED talk site helps students to understand their roles as presenters/educators, audience/concerned citizens, film crew/documentation to archive the work for others to view.

It is also worth considering if you want the student TED talks to be in a more formal setting or in a less formal setting. A more formal setting matches the TED talk mentors the students studied. A less formal setting supports the ongoing work students are familiar with from previous units of study. Both formal and informal TED talk settings are easy to set up. For a more formal setting, we suggest using a backdrop made from a roll of craft paper or bulletin board paper, a simple "TED" sign for the backdrop, and a small red rug for the presenters to stand on. For a less formal setting, we suggest a small table for presenters to sit or stand behind as they give their TED talk.

Here's a tip: This session works best if you give students 7–10 minutes to set up at the start of the period for presenters to get their supports ready, for documentor(s) to set up their devices to film, and for audience members to set up their notebooks to engage in the TED talk presentations. Once you begin, you can expect the TED talk presentations to run in five-minute intervals: three minutes for presentation with remaining two minutes for next group to set up, for documentor(s) to upload, for fellow researchers to reflect in their notebooks, and for presenters to complete the self-assessment checklist.

It's important to set up what kids are doing when they are not filming. One clear option is for study groups to be paired with other study groups who are watching, and then giving specific, complimentary feedback such as:

- the most compelling points

- interesting techniques (visuals, anecdotes, and other craft techniques)

- powerful presentation moves

- new thinking they led their audience to.

It is helpful to prep students on how to be an audience member: making eye contact, smiling, nodding in agreement, matching the mood, studying the visuals, being open to new and possibly challenging information, jotting notes. Kids need support in listening to each other carefully and in the kind of feedback they give. Critical feedback is not that helpful at this point. Complimentary feedback on parts that went well is very helpful.

You may also want to provide students with a tool for self-assessment (and you can use it for assessment as well). Consider the skills that are important to kids' ongoing growth, and note those. Here's an example, that's also available in the online resources—as a Word document so you can tinker with it. Some of you may want to change the self-assessment columns, for instance, to AS (approaching standard), MS (meets standard), ES (exceeds standards).

TED-Style Talks	Somewhat	Consistently	Yes!
We spoke about our topic with passion and zeal, inspiring our audience to care.			
We synthesized information from our research, highlighting big ideas, and linking details to support these ideas.			
We used visuals to make our presentation more compelling.			
We used academic vocabulary that is significant to this study, and explained it as needed.			

TED-Style Talks	Somewhat	Consistently	Yes!
Our presentation showed evidence of rehearsal and reflection (fluency in presentation, use of supports such as visuals and sources, questioning, and connections).			
We acknowledged important sources by referring to authors or texts inside of the presentation.			

If you decide to collect kids' notebooks at the end of the unit, you may want to draw once again on the Research Notebooks rubric you introduced early on in the unit. You may also want to invite kids to assess their own notebook work, and to reflect upon how much their notebook worked changed from the beginning to the end of the unit.

Finally, friends, remember to think about celebrating the work you've done. You might invite some colleagues or families or students in other classes in for your students' talks. Your students might offer to mentor other students in research, flash-debate, and giving talks—and in study habits. Definitely invite students to talk a bit about how their thinking and research have changed over time. We've included a short video of some students talking this way, in the online resources for this unit. It's just so beautiful to hear kids speak about how they used to think . . . but now they think . . .

And take a moment to celebrate your own teaching. We know that the energy of the teacher is what directly inspires students. You believing in kids becoming more powerful is the best gift you can give your students. Thank you for your care, for your belief, for the work that you do.

All the best,
Marc and Mary

Notebook Checklist			
Research Notebooks	Somewhat	Consistently	Yes!
1. I've kept track of sources, developing a system that let's me return to texts and reference them accurately			
2. I've developed a system for collecting significant vocabulary terms and concepts			
3. I've gone back into my notes, annotating, re-organizing, synthesizing			
4. As my research progressed, I've taken deeper, more detailed notes, varying my note-taking structures to match my purpose			
5. My notes show evidence of how my thinking has developed and changed over time - writing to think, reflection, analysis			
6. My research notes show the fairness of my research - I have researched multiple perspectives			
7. My notes indicate process toward my project - study of mentor texts, suggestions from my study group, preparation for Ted Talk			